WALLACE MENDELSON

CAPITALISM, DEMOCRACY, AND THE SUPREME COURT

CURRENT POLITICAL PROBLEMS

CIVIL LIBERTIES

CAPITALISM, DEMOCRACY, AND THE SUPREME COURT

CURRENT POLITICAL PROBLEMS

TAYLOR COLE, EDITOR

Civil Liberties

WALLACE MENDELSON, *Capitalism, Democracy, and the Supreme Court*

GEORGE W. SPICER, *The Supreme Court and Fundamental Freedoms*

In preparation

JOHN H. HALLOWELL, *Man's Search for Freedom*

ROBERT S. RANKIN, *Civil Liberties and Martial Law*

CAPITALISM, DEMOCRACY, AND THE SUPREME COURT

Wallace Mendelson
THE UNIVERSITY OF TEXAS

NEW YORK
APPLETON-CENTURY-CROFTS, INC.

640–1

Library of Congress Card number: 60–10146

PRINTED IN THE UNITED STATES OF AMERICA

For

Rose and Harry Rosen

in appreciation

PREFACE

A nation cannot live by bread alone—neither can it thrive solely on spiritual rations. American experience suggests that the interplay of material and ideal forces is the matrix of history. Governor Winthrop of the Massachusetts Bay Colony was not speaking from an ivory tower when he dubbed democracy "the worst of all forms of Government" and proclaimed that "God Almightie . . . hath soe disposed the condition of mankinde, as in all times some must be rich, some poore. . . ." * The clashes between Hamilton and Jefferson, between Biddle and Jackson, were of the same stuff that made Lincoln exalt "the man above the dollar," led Woodrow Wilson to challenge Big Business, and Franklin Roosevelt to speak of driving the money-changers out of the temple. Paine, Jefferson, Jackson, Lincoln, Bryan, Wilson, and the New Deal represent one tradition—just as Winthrop, Hamilton, Biddle, Grant, McKinley, Harding, and the Tafts represent another. In general the difference between them is a difference in view as to the relation between popular government and private enterprise, between democracy and capitalism. The purpose of this little book is to trace in broad outline the impact of these forces upon American constitutional law.

It is a pleasure to acknowledge the generous permission of the copyright holders to quote from the following books: Harcourt, Brace and Company, Inc., *Main Currents in American Thought* by V. L. Parrington; Alfred A. Knopf, Incorporated, *The American Experience* by H. B. Parkes; and the Ronald Press Company, *The Course of American Democratic Thought* by R. H. Gabriel.

I have also drawn with kind permission from the copyright holders upon my own previous writing, as follows: "Dred Scott's Case—Reconsidered," 38 *Minnesota Law Review* 16 (1953); "Mr. Justice Holmes—Humility, Skepticism and Democracy," 36 *Minnesota Law Review* 343 (1952); "Chief Justice Taney—Jacksonian

* Quoted in Alpheus T. Mason and Richard H. Leach, *In Quest of Freedom: American Political Thought and Practice* (Englewood Cliffs, N.J., Prentice-Hall, Inc., 1959), p. 28.

Judge," 12 *University of Pittsburgh Law Review* 381 (1951); "Mr. Justice Field and Laissez Faire," 36 *Virginia Law Review* 45 (1950); "Chief Justice Marshall and the Mercantile Tradition," 29 *The Southwestern Social Science Quarterly* 27 (1948).

CONTENTS

CAPITALISM, DEMOCRACY, AND THE SUPREME COURT

I

PROLOGUE

Mercantilism was the bridge between feudalism and modern capitalism. By the close of the Middle Ages, Europe had tamed her barbarian invaders, and was safe again for widespread economic intercourse. The resulting commercial revolution produced a new social phenomenon: the middle class and its urban habitat. The bourgeoisie sponsored and used absolute monarchy as a weapon to destroy church, feudal and guild interference with trade. Political philosophy explained in terms of "sovereignty." The special consideration which the new monarchs gave their middle class sponsors was called the mercantile system.

Though its tactics varied with time and place, mercantilism was always in essence a policy of national economic integration. It found negative expression in efforts to overcome feudal particularism and Roman cosmopolitanism. Its positive element was special encouragement for national trade and industry. As Schmoller emphasized, the mercantile system was simply "town policy writ large." It marked the transition from local to national economies. The sovereign nation-state gave merchants larger and safer market areas. It was also their weapon against the anti-business bias of both feudalism and the Roman Church.

By the end of the eighteenth century the businessman-leader of the middle class had replaced feudal lord and ecclesiastic at the social center of gravity. Gold instead of land became the measure of value. Weber and Tawney have traced the rise and triumph of the new moral code which made cardinal virtues of hard work, thrift, and business success. Profits replaced salvation as the goal of life on earth. Science incidentally was freed from medieval superstition and the deductive mode of reasoning. Law, always rationalizing dominant social trends, bent to meet bourgeois needs. On the continent feudal and canon jurisprudence gave way to the Reception of Roman law. The sophisticated concepts of sovereignty, property and contract of ancient commercial Rome suited mercantile needs far better than did feudal land law or the Church's strictures on property and business. In the famous phrase of Sir Henry Maine, contract replaced status as the foundation of social rights and duties. That is to say, allodial replaced feudal tenure of property.

In England the more pliable, hence tougher, common law accommodated the new needs. Particularly under Lords Holt and Mansfield it absorbed strong doses of the Law Merchant and even some Roman law doctrines. For the first time the law of England became truly national, and served thereby the nation-state. The most radical change came in property law. By the end of the eighteenth century the medieval principle that "man ought to possess external things not as his own but as common" [1] was dead. The great popularizer Blackstone could say, "so great is the regard of the Law for private property, that it will not authorize the least violation of it; no, not even for the common good of the whole community." [2]

This revolutionary concept of property, its corollary—freedom of contract—and the sovereign nation-state were institutional expressions of the revival of trade at the close of the Middle Ages. Through them, Western civilization was transformed to meet the needs of the business middle class. That is the essence of English Mercantilism, French Colbertism and German Cameralism. But as Adam Smith said, "It cannot be very difficult to determine who have been the contrivers of this whole mercantile system; not the consumers, we may believe, whose interest has been entirely neglected; but the producers, whose interest has been so carefully attended to; and among this latter class our merchants and manufacturers have been by far the principal architects." [3] Having

[1] Thomas Aquinas, *Summa Theologica* (London, Burns Oates & Washbourne, 1929), Vol. 10, pp. 221–222.

[2] *Commentaries on the Laws of England,* W. C. Jones, ed. (San Francisco, Bancroft-Whitney, 1916), Vol. 1, p. 240.

[3] *The Wealth of Nations,* 5th ed., E. Cannan ed. (London, Methuen, 1930), Vol. 2, p. 160.

attained freedom from church, feudal and later royal [4] interference from above, the businessman soon found his way of life threatened from below. The lower classes were taking literally and pressing against him his own claims to liberty and equality. In opposition to popes, barons, and finally kings, the business class had philosophized in universal terms; but time revealed that the freedoms it sought were fashioned for its own peculiar business needs. This discrepancy explains the difference between the Old and the New Whigs, Bentham's life-long battle against Blackstone, and resistance to the Reform Bills. Macaulay, for example, feared broad suffrage would jeopardize private property [5]—"the great institution for the sake of which chiefly all other institutions exist, the great institution to which we owe all knowledge, all commerce, all industry, all civilization. . . ."

Early American history is largely a special chapter in the general progress of the business middle class, its concepts of nationalism, property and contract, and its defenses against interference from above and unrest from below. For generations prior to 1776, each of the thirteen colonies was torn by rivalry between the back country and the Atlantic fringe. The coastal plain in the north from New Hampshire to Pennsylvania was dedicated to commerce and industry. Here lay the urban centers with their powerful mercantile families. The tidewater region to the south from Maryland to Georgia was the province of the great planters. Charleston was its only important city. Inland from New England to Georgia ranged a fringe of frontier settlements—"the old West." This was the land of the small, pioneer farmer, the seat of indigenous American democracy. Its radical, new-world outlook offended the conservative, Europe-bound culture of the sea-coast. Though the West grew much more rapidly, the East controlled colonial legislatures. Then, as now, those who dominate lawmaking assemblies were not inclined to surrender control by reapportionment. The resulting political imbalance brought unfair tax burdens and an effective legislative veto—supplemented, if need be, by a royal veto—upon Western aspirations. Seated near the ocean and

[4] When the absolute monarch had served his purpose as liquidator of feudal and church restraints on trade, the middle class turned upon him with constitutionalism and laissez-faire.

[5] Speech on the Reform Bill in the House of Commons, May 3, 1842.

coastal waterways, merchants and planters were slow to provide roads and bridges which farmers needed to market their crops. Safe behind a barrier of frontier farms, they were niggardly in appropriating money for protection against Indians. Indeed, it has been suggested that merchants in the fur trade were more interested in protecting Indians from frontiersmen. Legislative domination gave Easterners an enormous advantage in land speculation. This tended to keep the frontiersman land-hungry and in debt to Eastern speculators. Thus cultural and political tensions were aggravated by debtor-creditor grievances, including the classic argument over soft versus hard money.

When the burden became too great, backwoodsmen were quite capable of revolt, as in Bacon's Rebellion in Virginia, the Regulator outburst in the Carolinas, the land bank controversy in Massachusetts, the tenant farmer eruptions in New York and New Jersey and later the Shays' and Whiskey Rebellions.

With this background, the American Revolution inevitably entailed more than a military contest between a mother country and her colonies. It was also a struggle for power between the merchant-planter oligarchy of the sea-coast and the radical, democratic Western frontiersman. As a famous spokesman for the former observed, "When the pot boils, the scum rises." The "scum" referred to included, of course, not only Western yeomen, but also Eastern urban workers insisting upon wider economic opportunity and political rights. In the eyes of the common man—whether of the city or the frontier—the ruling classes at home were supported by, and hardly better than, the British oligarchy. Thus the struggle for colonial democracy merged into the struggle for freedom from England. It was not a Marxian clash between those who held property and those who did not. Farmers, by far the largest group in America, were just as property-conscious as their merchant and planter counterparts. City workers were anxious to acquire property as well as political rights. The American domestic revolution had cultural, sectional, and political, as well as economic facets.

Northern merchants, of course, suffered most directly from the new British colonial policies that arose at the end of the Seven Years' War in 1763. Yet as a class they were least inclined toward independence. The golden business advantages of membership in the British mercantile empire were great and obvious. Merchants' needs were best served by negotiation calculated to insure the continued benefits of membership in the Empire with freedom from imperial taxes. Their charges against London accordingly were petty-fogging and legalistic. James Otis argued that writs of assistance violated the *British Constitution*. The argument against taxation without representation was both unfounded and futile. Logically it entailed sending colonial representatives to Parliament, where they would be hopelessly outvoted. When the Stamp Act was adopted, some tried to distinguish between Parliament's power to levy "external" and "internal" taxes. When the British sought to humor the colonials by repealing the "internal" Stamp Act in favor of the "external" Townshend Acts, John Dickinson's answer was another distinction, this time between taxation and regulation. When this failed, James Wilson sought to distinguish between allegiance to the Crown (which had no power to tax or regulate) and allegiance to Parliament (which had those powers).[6]

For such quibbles Western and urban radicals like Patrick Henry and Sam Adams charged the merchants and their lawyers with half-hearted opposition to the British. "Shall we Proteus-like perpetually change our ground, assume every moment some new strange shape, to defend, to evade?" When legal dialectics failed, the merchant princes resorted to the "scum" for support and thereby eventually lost control of the revolution. City mobs stoned and intimidated royal officials, burned custom collectors' boats, dumped tea, and provoked British troops into the "Boston Massacre." At the intellectual level the argument shifted from the British Constitution and the Rights of Englishmen to Natural Law and the Rights of Man. But such views, justifying and supported by mob action, were as dangerous to the colonial oligarchy as to the English. Feeling themselves pushed too far, conservatives sought reconciliation. In 1774, Gouverneur Morris, a wealthy lawyer-merchant-banker, declared that if the dispute with Britain continued, America would be ruled by a riotous mob. Many who for a time supported the cause of protest drew back when they saw the extremes to which some were prepared to go. "Between the radicals and the conservatives," wrote Van Tyne, "the chasm was

[6] The shifting argument is traced in Carl Becker, *The Declaration of Independence* (New York, Smith Peter, 1922), Ch. 3.

widening. Just as each new act of war or wild rumor made reconciliation with England less likely, so untoward events and words spoken in rage made civil war between Whig and Tory inevitable."[7] Joseph Galloway argued that if Parliament had no authority in the colonies, they would be in "a perfect state of nature," i.e., anarchy. Civil War would be inevitable. This, he insisted, could be avoided only by the presence of British authority. Men like Robert Morris, John Dickinson and James Duane fully agreed.

So evenly balanced were the radical and conservative forces in the First Continental Congress that Galloway's plan for "reunion" with the mother country failed by only one vote. Even after blood had been spilled at Lexington and Concord, the Second Continental Congress could not accept war and declare independence without severe resistance. Conservatives, led by John Dickinson, fought for conciliation and succeeded in passing yet another Olive Branch Petition to the king. As late as 1775, Congress declared that "We mean not to dissolve that union which has so long and so happily existed between us. . . . We have not raised armies with ambitious designs of separating from Great Britain, and establishing independent States. . . ." Even in the fall of 1775 five colonial legislatures dominated by conservatives voted against independence. As late as January, 1776, the officers' mess over which General Washington presided toasted the king's health each evening.

Then ordinary people made up their minds. The decisive factor was Tom Paine's *Common Sense*. Published in January, 1776, its total sales soon exceeded half a million copies. Paine swept aside legalistic subtleties and lingering sentiments in a common sense appeal to the economic self-interest of the American people—and the principle of popular sovereignty. It was not a debate, but a rousing call for independence, a denunciation of monarchy and all that it stood for in the lives of ordinary citizens. Here was a man of the people speaking the common tongue. Even the rare conservative, like John Adams who had worked for independence from the beginning, could not accept the "filthy," "atheistic" Tom Paine with his ideal of popular sovereignty. Conservatives did not mean to free themselves from one set of masters only

[7] See Claude H. Van Tyne, *The American Revolution* (New York, Harper, 1905), Ch. 4 and 5.

to be subjected to another. Far from objecting to the English oligarchic class system, they admired and strove to perpetuate it in America. They resented the mercantile policies of George III and his ministers, not because they disliked mercantilism, but because they were not its chief beneficiaries. "The American Revolution," wrote Millen Chamberlain, "was not a quarrel between two peoples . . . it was a strife between two parties, the conservatives in both countries in one party, and the liberals in both countries as the other party."

Of course, the domestic struggle between these forces did not end with independence. Both the first and the second American constitutions bear the mark of their rivalry. The conservatives were led by Robert Morris, John Jay, James Wilson, Gouverneur Morris, Alexander Hamilton, Henry Knox, George Washington, James Duane, John Adams, John Dickinson, Edmund Randolph, and C. C. Pinckney. These "natural leaders" of an eighteenth-century, British-oriented, old-world social order deeply distrusted the common man and his capacity to govern himself. John Jay put their view succinctly, "The people who own the country ought to govern it." [8] Hamilton called them and their followers the party of the "rich and the well-born." [9] Government had always been in the hands of a small, wealthy few, backed by the whole weight of social, religious, economic and political convention. Eighteenth century conservatives believed it could never be in any other hands. They were, after all, hard-headed practical men of affairs, not "theorists." They believed in strong central government as the only sure restraint upon the "rabble." They put great store in executive and judicial authority as a check upon popular assemblies. If eventually they became radical in their attitude towards England, they were horrified by anything that smacked of democracy. To destroy what Ostrogorski called "the old unity"—a hierarchy of classes bound together by mutual interdependence and time-honored social ties—was to destroy society itself. If the masses were to be freed from their old masters what would hold society and the state together? Conservatives in short were motivated by fear, not by hope. They

[8] Quoted in Richard Hofstadter, *The American Political Tradition* (New York, Vintage, 1954), pp. 15–16.

[9] *The Records of the Federal Convention of 1787*, Max Farrand, ed. (New Haven, Yale U.P., 1937), Vol. 1, pp. 299–300.

saw the common man as neither virtuous nor rational, but as ignorant, incompetent and inclined to violence. It followed that, if government were to be stable, it must be dominated as from time immemorial by those whose position and property gave them a special "stake in society."

The leaders of the radical opposition were Thomas Jefferson, Sam Adams, Benjamin Franklin, Tom Paine, Christopher Gadsden, Patrick Henry, Richard Henry Lee, George Clinton, James Warren, Samuel and George Bryan. As a group these men were guided more by hope than by fear. They had greater faith in the common people than did their opponents. Their reading of history, reinforced by experience with Britain, made them skeptical of strong central authority. For them the future lay in local self-government with annually elected popular assemblies free of "aristocratic" interference by judges and executives. Some of the "radicals" were men of wealth; all respected private property. But few, if any, shared that overbearing regard for pecuniary values which seemed so prominent among their conservative opponents. Respect for property did not blind them to the rights of man and the public welfare. According to Franklin,[10]

> All the property that is necessary to a man, for the conservation of the individual and the propagation of the species, is his natural right, which none can justly deprive him of: but all property superfluous to such purposes is the property of the public, who by their laws have created it, and who may therefore by other laws dispose of it, whenever the welfare of the public shall demand such disposition.

Jefferson put the matter in a thimble.[11]

> Men, according to their constitutions, and the circumstances in which they are placed, differ honestly in opinion. Some are Whigs, Liberals, Democrats, call them what you please. Others are Tories, Serviles, Aristocrats, etc. The latter fear the people, and wish to transfer all power to the higher classes of society; the former consider the people as the safest depository of power in the last resort. . . .

[10] Quoted in Avery Craven and Walter Johnson, *The United States, Experiment in Democracy* (New York, Ginn, 1952), p. 111.

[11] Quoted in Arthur M. Schlesinger, *New Viewpoints in American History* (New York, Macmillan, 1922), p. 404.

Hamilton's "Your people, Sir, is a great beast" rings down through the ages along with Jefferson's "the common sense of the common people is the greatest and soundest force on earth."

In the revolutionary era from 1776 to 1787, the Jeffersonians were dominant. They achieved their goal of independence, abolished primogeniture and entail (the legal foundation of a landed aristocracy), eliminated established churches in six of the ten states which had had them, made some progress against slavery and the slave trade, and procured new state constitutions featuring bills of rights, extending suffrage, and exalting annually elected "popular" assemblies at the expense of executives and courts. Yet everywhere resistance was great. Forces anything but democratic by modern standards seem to have retained control in most states. But in the eyes of that day's conservatives the innovations seemed outrageous.

At the national level, liberalism unquestionably carried the day. Just as conservatives were reluctant to shake off British government, so they were fast to demand centralized government at home. In their view, independence could not be achieved without first establishing a strong national government. Centralized authority to veto state action, to enact general legislation, and to suppress rebellion died with the Declaration of Independence. These were indispensable to the conservative cause. If John Dickinson held out to the sour end for reconciliation with the crown, he was the first to devise a plan for central authority at home to replace it. His initial draft of the Articles of Confederation in 1776 called for ultimate legal authority in a national government. States could control matters of their "internal police" *where such control did not interfere with national authority. The residue of power—with one severe, typically conservative, restraint on taxation—was given to the central government.*

Though the plan was couched in obscure terms, it did not fool the liberals. They saw it for what it was designed to be—and rerejected it. As Andrew McLaughlin observed, the old problem of imperial organization, of striking a balance between the whole and its parts, had now crossed the ocean. What finally emerged from the Second Continental Congress was a complete victory for local self-government. Specified and limited "powers" were given to Congress. The residue was for the states. There was little or no executive or judicial authority, and nothing that could be construed to make central authority supreme vis-a-vis either states or individuals. In sum, no central government at all was established. State sovereignty reigned supreme. The Articles of Confederation as finally adopted in 1781 were not the child of ignorance or inexperience. They were a pure expression of the same revolutionary ideal that led to independence. There would be no point in substituting one far-off centralized authority for another. Local self-government, unhampered by executive and judicial interference, was the progressive ideal of the day. "Checks and balances"—like remote super-government—was for those who feared the people. It is only a surface paradox that generations later conservatives resorted to "States rights"—after the common man had got control of national government.

Having achieved their goal, the liberals disbanded, and—temporarily—lost their victory. The opposition, a much smaller and more homogeneous group, remained organized and active. They sugar-coated their objective by calling themselves Federalists rather than nationalists. Temperament or economic interest led them to favor

> executive and judicial rather than legislative control of state and central governments, . . . rigorous collection of [regressive] taxes, and, as creditors, . . . strict payment of public and private debts. They declared that national honor and prestige could be maintained only by powerful central government. Naturally, not all men who used such language used it sincerely, for some were as selfish as their opponents said they were. The nationalists frankly disliked the political heritage of the Revolution. They deplored the fact that there was no check upon the actions of majorities in state legislatures; that there was no central government to which minorities could appeal from the decisions of such majorities, as they had done before the Revolution.[12]

Their cause was enormously helped by a depression that followed the war and the economic shock of sudden severance from the integrated, world-wide British economy. Hard times brought tax strikes and state efforts to ease the pressures on the poor by such devices as paper money and "stay laws" against precipitous mortgage foreclosures. Judicial intervention on behalf of creditors provoked both legislative and mob reprisals against courts. States

[12] Merrill Jensen, *The New Nation* (New York, Knopf, 1950), p. 425.

in a position to do so imposed interstate trade barriers for local advantage at the expense of the general welfare. More than one of them refused to respect national treaties. Shays' Rebellion was the final blow.

For conservatives all this flowed from "the evils of democracy." Playing up the difficulty of the times for all, and perhaps more than, it was worth, they proposed and got a convention *to revise the Articles of Confederation.* Hamilton led the movement. It was composed largely of those who had held out longest against independence and who had fought hardest for Dickinson's first draft of the Articles. Excepting the aged Franklin, not one of the great, popular instigators of independence joined them. Patrick Henry had been chosen to attend, but refused because in his own words he "smelt a rat" in such an elite gathering of the gentry. And so the Constitutional Convention lost the one famous delegate who directly represented the way of life of most Americans: the small farmers and frontiersmen of the old West. Virtually all others were merchants and planters, or their legal spokesmen—representing in a direct sense the life and experience of less than 10 per cent of the American people.

Surely it is significant that the Constitutional Convention of 1787 held its discussions in secret. Apparently the democratic Franklin was suspect. Tradition has it that he was permitted to dine out only in the company of less talkative—that is, more reliable—members. Small wonder! Edmond Randolph set the convention's tone in his opening speech, "our chief danger arises from the democratic parts of our constitutions. . . . None of the [state] constitutions have provided a sufficient check against democracy." [13] James McHenry thought democracy was synonymous with "confusion and licentiousness." [14] J. F. Mercer objected "to the mode of election by the people. The people cannot know and judge of the character of candidates. The worst possible choice will be made." "The people," said John Sherman, "immediately should have as little to do as may be about the government. They want information and are constantly liable to be misled." Oliver Ellsworth dis-

[13] Farrand, *op. cit.*, Vol. 1, pp. 26–27.

[14] The language quoted here and in the remainder of this paragraph is quoted in Charles A. Beard, *An Economic Interpretation of the Constitution of the United States* (New York, Macmillan, 1944) pp. 194–214.

trusted "leveling democracy." Finding a "dangerous thirst after more power in some of our legislatures," William Livingston thought "a negative in the hands of the executive and judicial powers is absolutely necessary. . . ." John Dickinson regarded a "limited monarchy as one of the best governments in the world. . . . It was certain that equal blessings had never yet been derived from any republican form." Elbridge Gerry proclaimed that "the evils we experience flow from an excess of democracy."

It is easy to misunderstand the Convention's members, if one insists upon seeing them in twentieth-century terms. Admittedly, as Madison recognized, their purpose was to "protect the minority of the opulent" against the majority. But this does not mean they believed in dictatorship. Nor do they appear to have been consciously motivated by crude selfishness or ambition:[15]

> What determined their decisions was not their own economic interests, but the political attitudes and ideals into which they had been educated. *** Differing from the agrarians in their conceptions of freedom and property rights, they regarded it as almost self-evident that the direct rule of the ignorant masses was dangerous and that the country should be guided by an elite of "gentlemen of principle and property."

Such an attitude is understandable, yet it had little basis in reality. The masses of whom they were afraid were not the oppressed proletariat and peasantry of Europe, but the free and independent property-owning farmers of America. And perhaps the most striking characteristic of these eighteenth century merchants and planters was that they still thought largely in European terms. The American society of that epoch was unique; but there was as yet no developed theory of government, even among the agrarians, that took account of its unique features. So both for warnings of what to avoid and for models to be imitated, the members of the convention turned to the history of European countries, ancient and contemporary, quoting extensive precedents from the experience of Greece, Rome, Holland, Germany, Poland, and Great Britain. When they shuddered at the dangers of mob rule, they were thinking of ancient city-states and of the mobs of London and Paris, not of the independent proprietors who composed the chief democratic element in America. And when they were horrified by Shays' Rebellion, they were identifying it with European class struggles; they did not sufficiently

[15] Henry B. Parkes, *The American Experience* (New York, Knopf, 1955), pp. 121–122.

recognize that the farmers responsible for the rebellion were fighting not for the destruction of all property rights, but for the right to keep property of their own. . . . There was much truth in words written a number of years later by Thomas Jefferson. "It must be agreed," he declared, "that our governments have much less of republicanism than ought to have been expected; in other words, that the people have less regular control . . . than their rights and interests require. And this I ascribe not to any want of republican dispositions in those who formed these Constitutions, but to a submission of true principles to European authorities . . . whose fears of the people have been inspired by the populace of their own great cities, and were unjustly entertained against the independent, the happy, and therefore orderly citizens of the United States."

In short, on major points the delegates were in substantial agreement: democracy and States' rights were a curse. After all, in their view it was the states that had succumbed to "the evils of democracy." Hamilton proposed the obvious solution: abolition of the states in favor of national government with a strong oligarchic caste. Less forthright delegates saw that such proposals had no chance of acceptance. Conservatives had learned some lessons. Colonel Mason put the dilemma neatly. "Notwithstanding the oppression and injustice experienced among us from democracy, the genius of the people is in favor of it, and the genius of the people must be consulted." [16] The result was compromise—at least semantically. Oligarchy at one extreme and democracy at the other were rejected in favor of "republicanism." The extremes of nationalism and state sovereignty were rejected in favor of "federalism." We need not be fooled by the terminology. In fact, the Federalists carried the day. Violating their authority, they offered not amendments to the Articles, but an entirely new system. Under their proposals, democracy would have small quarter. Of the four proposed new agencies of government—President, courts, Senate and House—only one was directly chosen by the people. An elaborate system of staggered terms and checks and balances foreclosed any possibility of direct popular control. Plainly the tightly organized Federalists, relying upon the power of talents, prestige and wealth, expected to take control of the new government—as in fact they did. The machinery was made for operation by an oligarchy and

[16] Quoted in Vernon L. Parrington, *Main Currents in American Thought* (New York, Harcourt, Brace, 1927), Vol. 1, pp. 281–282.

was so operated—*until Jefferson found its Achilles heel.* Moreover, it was made to supercede the states at least in areas important to conservatives. States were forbidden to impair the obligations of contracts (for example via "stay laws"), issue paper money, make debts payable in anything but gold or silver coin, or to impose specified burdens upon commerce (Article I, Sec. 10). Here was a bill of rights for business, though of course there was none for the great democratic freedoms of speech, press and religion. On the affirmative side, the Constitution gave the new government fiscal independence and extensive authority, including power to promote and protect both domestic and foreign commerce (Article I, Sec. 8). Finally, in its broad, because loosely defined, sphere of action federal authority was made supreme, "anything in the Constitution or laws of any State to the contrary notwithstanding" (Article VI, Sec. 2).

If the conservatives made linguistic concessions, surely the original Constitution gave them the heart of what they wanted; hence the potent and almost successful popular resistance to ratification. The three most prominent leaders of the movement for independence—Samuel Adams, Patrick Henry, and Richard Henry Lee—opposed the Constitution for the same reasons that they had opposed Britain. They resented remote, centralized, oligarchic government. To save America from it, Lee had introduced the motion for independence in the Second Continental Congress. Recognizing some desirable features in the Constitution, he could not accept the absence of "that one important factor of free government, a representation of the people." "Every man of reflection," he held, "must see that the change now proposed is a transfer of power from the many to the few." [17] Similarly Patrick Henry said,[18] "I look upon that paper [the Constitution] as the most fatal plan that could possibly be conceived to enslave a free people."

The ratification fight was bitter and close. Indeed, we have it on John Marshall's authority: [19]

[17] Richard H. Lee, "Letters from the Federal Farmer to the Republican," in *Pamphlets on the Constitution of the United States,* P. L. Ford, ed. (Brooklyn, 1888), pp. 317–318.

[18] Patrick Henry led the antiratification fight in Virginia. See Hugh B. Grigsby, *The History of the Virginia Federal Convention of 1788* (Richmond, Virginia Historical Society, 1890), pp. 80–81 and *passim.*

[19] *Life of Washington* (Philadelphia, Wayne, 1807), Vol. 5, p. 132.

> So balanced were the parties in some of [the states] that even after the subject had been discussed for a considerable time, the fate of the Constitution could scarcely be conjectured; and so small in many instances, was the majority in its favor, as to afford strong ground for the opinion that, had the influence of character been removed, the intrinsic merits of the instrument would not have secured its adoption. Indeed it is scarcely to be doubted that in some of the adopting states a majority of the people were in opposition. In all of them, the numerous amendments proposed demonstrate the reluctance with which the new government was accepted; and that a dread of dismemberment, not an approbation of the particular system under consideration, had induced an acquiescence in it. . . .

This from an ardent Federalist supporter of ratification!

Compelled to concede a Bill of Rights, the Federalists got the Constitution and control of the new government as well. One Amos Singletary had predicted: [20]

> These lawyers, and men of learning, and monied men, that talk so finely, and gloss over matters so smoothly, to make us, poor illiterate people, swallow down the pill, expect to get into Congress themselves; they expect to be the managers of this Constitution, and get all the power and money into their own hands, and then they will swallow up all us little folk, like the great Leviathan.

From the popular point of view this prediction was not wide of the mark. Hamilton had become the leader of the Federalists and plainly the brains of the Washington administration. The Constitution created a nation on parchment. Hamilton tried to make it a nation in fact by the same devices that all other nation-builders of that era had used—by binding in economic allegiance to the central government the rising forces of the commercial revolution. In his own words, no society could prosper "which did not unite the interest and credit of rich individuals with those of the state." The goal of his statesmanship was to "make it the immediate interest of the monied men to co-operate with government in its support." [21] This marriage of economics and political power had been Colbert's goal in France, the Cameralist objective in Germany, and the essence of English Mercantilism. Hamilton's Federalism was a faith-

20 Parrington, *op. cit.*, Vol. 1, p. 284.

21 *Works of Alexander Hamilton*, H. C. Lodge, ed. (New York, Putnam, 1904), Vol. 3, pp. 332, 338.

ful replica of the British system, with one obvious modification: its primary beneficiaries were now to be the American, rather than the British, commercial classes. It found concrete expression in assumption of state obligations and funding of the national debt ("to raise around the administration a moneyed aristocracy" comparable to the rentiers raised by the British consolidated debt first funded in 1751); establishment of a national bank (inspired by the Bank of England) and "hard" money (both of these to serve especially commercial interests); an army and a navy (to control future Shaysites and to protect maritime commerce); trade restrictions in favor of American shippers; and, after the outbreak of the French Revolution, a pro-British foreign policy. All this of course was financed by a thoroughly regressive revenue system—tariff and whiskey tax—the burden of which inevitably fell most heavily upon the non-commercial classes.[22]

In the Constitutional Convention, Hamilton had argued that all communities are made up of two classes. "The first are the rich and the well born, the other the mass of the people. . . . The people are turbulent and changing; they seldom judge or determine right. Give therefore to the first class a distinct and permanent share in the government [by institutions not unlike a king and a house of lords]." [23] This was no longer feasible, as even the Federalists had recognized. Yet the special stake in government for the "rich and the well born" that Hamilton could not win in the Convention, he achieved as Washington's "prime minister."

Just as British mercantilism led non-favored groups to revolt, so did that of the Federalists. Hamilton had grossly favored commercial interests. Southerners and Westerners with some help from the urban masses soon found a spokesman in Thomas Jefferson. They repudiated the thought that America must resort to old-world expedients—a glorified system of government bounties to purchase the support of the influential few. Inspired by the idealism of the French Revolution and the new English economic revolt called "laissez faire," they sought reform at home. The American Revolution was not yet complete. But how could it be peacefully

[22] The Whiskey Tax was particularly burdensome to frontier farmers who converted their bulky grain to more easily transported liquor for market purposes.

[23] Farrand, *op. cit.*, Vol. 1, pp. 299–300.

achieved? Within Washington's cabinet Jefferson had vainly opposed every element of Hamilton's program. Thanks to the elaborate "check and balance" system, attack from outside promised equal futility. Yet surely there was some way to circumvent the elaborate constitutional devices designed to insulate the national government from direct popular control. Jefferson found it in the political party system. Here was his great institutional gift to American democracy. If the old order was to be shattered, if common men were to be free of their traditional upper-class masters, they must organize for self-government, or flounder helplessly in atomistic isolation. Popular government could never have been achieved under "checks and balances" along with the Federalist no-party—read one-party—system. Thus in 1791 Jefferson resigned from the cabinet to organize a popular opposition party.

It is not by chance that Washington's Farewell Address—written by Hamilton—warned against political "factions." In the Federalist view there could "be but two parties in a country, the friends of order and its foes." When repeated admonitions of this type failed, the Federalists overreached themselves in the Alien and Sedition Acts. These were aimed at the foreign "isms" of the French Revolution—that is, democracy—and at Jeffersonian criticism of Federalist government. The idea of a loyal, organized opposition—the essence of the political party system—was beyond the vision of eighteenth century conservatives. When they used the Sedition Act for partisan purposes to prosecute a number of Jefferson's lieutenants, the American people rebelled. A "revolution at the polls" in 1800 swept the high-toned, old-world Federalists out of office to a lingering death. After an hiatus of a dozen years the forces of new-world liberalism were back in power. Before Jefferson left office, the Twelfth Amendment constitutionalized the two-party system to avoid repetition of the election imbroglios of 1796 and 1800.

"Hamilton had a vision of the future of the United States that was at once too innocent for his mercenary fellow Federalists and too sophisticated for the 'new American' verging on the vast and wonderful frontier. Hamilton was concerned with money only as a medium for national, not personal aggrandizement; capital was the heart . . . of power; capitalists the instruments of progress; the state the directing force. But Federalist capitalists thought, as a rule, on a lower plane, and nursed their substance carefully in the familiar lines of investment." [24] If Federalists never ceased to admire British institutions and somewhat reluctantly adopted independence, they laid the foundations for effective national government—and then tarnished that contribution by resort to the Hartford Convention. Reluctantly accepting centralized authority, the Jeffersonians democratized it [25] and preserved important elements of local self-government. Then, generations later, they too changed their minds about national authority—when they discovered that in an industrial society it could serve their ends more effectively than could the states. Obviously parochialism and nationalism are merely means—used differently in different eras—to more abiding ends: Hamiltonianism and Jeffersonianism. These, it has been said, typify Goethe's two eternal spirits that contend for control of all human conduct: the spirit that denies, and the spirit that creates; the mocking doubt that human nature can ever change, and the hope that through the ages man can raise himself a little closer to perfection.[26] The interplay of these forces is a key to American history. The one produced and nourishes our distinctive moral strength: the ideal of human freedom and equality in a progressive social order unhampered by rigid class barriers. The other perhaps has made special contribution to our physical prowess through its emphasis upon business enterprise. The one emphasizes our spiritual, the other our material, standard of living. Reconciling them has been America's major preoccupation.

[24] William Miller, *A New History of the United States* (New York, Braziller, 1958), p. 134.

[25] First they gave us the Bill of Rights, then the party system and extension of the suffrage. Later they brought about the substantial bypassing of the electoral college so as to accomplish in effect the direct popular election of Presidents. Finally they instigated the direct election of Senators. Behind these developments, of course, lay the Jeffersonian ideology of democratic, self-government.

[26] Samuel E. Morison and Henry S. Commager, *The Growth of the American Republic,* 3rd ed. (New York, Oxford U.P., 1942), Vol. 1, p. 354.

II

CHIEF JUSTICE MARSHALL

Mercantilism

In the "lame duck" interval between the election of 1800 and the advent of the Jefferson administration, the Federalists expanded the jurisdiction of the national courts and packed them with staunch Federalist lawyers. John Marshall became Chief Justice. Hamilton had once dismissed the judiciary as "beyond comparison the weakest of the three departments"—but it was all that remained for the old regime. Could judges carry on from the bench the Hamiltonian policies that had been repudiated in 1800 by the "revolution at the polls"? Could mercantile nationalism be preserved as a bulwark against agrarian States-rights democracy?

Mr. Justice Holmes once remarked that "a great man represents a great ganglion in the nerves of society, or to vary the figure, a strategic point in the campaign of history, and part of his genius consists in being there." Hamilton had been *there* shaping the policies of Washington's administration. Marshall was to be his intellectual successor, though in a quite different office—one until his time deemed so unimportant as to be resigned by Ellsworth in favor of a diplomatic post and refused by Jay because he was "convinced that . . . [the Supreme Court] would not obtain the energy, weight, and dignity which are essential to its affording due support to the national government, or acquire the public confidence and respect which, as the last resort of the justice of the nation, it should possess."

There is perhaps poetic meaning in the fact that just as the original Federalist Constitution contained no Bill of Rights, so not one of Marshall's classic opinions vindicated any of the great civil liberties. Federalists had argued that no Bill of Rights was necessary since the national government had no power in any case to suppress such basic freedoms as speech, press and religion. This absence of power, however, did not deter them from passing the Sedition Act. Nor did it prevent Federalist Supreme Court Justices (sitting on circuit) from enforcing it viciously against anti-Federalist newspaper editors. Just as Jeffersonians gave us the Bill of Rights, so in this era it was they who had to enforce it —via Congress and the White House. President Jefferson pardoned all who had been convicted under the gag law and Congress repaid the fines. The Sedition Act never reached the Supreme Court. Doubtless its opponents were not anxious for it to get there, lest an unfortunate precedent be established. In their view, "the conduct of the Federal justices in the Sedition Act cases was a decisive argument against making the Supreme Court the final interpreter of the Constitution." [1]

Not only did Marshall's Court fail to vindicate any of the great democratic freedoms; its most famous effort—*Marbury v. Madison* [2]—asserted the supremacy of the judiciary vis-a-vis the politically responsible branches of the national government. This principle of "judicial review" was the ultimate conservative response to the "evils of democracy." If not expressly authorized in the Constitution, it had nevertheless long been a basic old-guard principle, accepted by most members of the Constitutional Convention and first publicly proclaimed by Hamilton.[3] After the Federalists lost control of the political branches, they became quite vocal on judicial review, particularly in the Great Debate on the Repeal Act of 1802.[4] This was the oligarchic answer to Jefferson's political party system. But in the Chase Impeachment, Jefferson seems to have had the last word. Never thereafter did Marshall or any member of his Court challenge another act of Congress. Of

[1] John C. Miller, *Crisis in Freedom* (Boston, Little Brown, 1951), pp. 138–139.

[2] 1 Cranch 137 (1803).

[3] See Carles A. Beard, *The Supreme Court and the Constitution* (New York, Paisley, 1938), p. 118; *The Federalist Papers,* Nos. 78 and 81.

[4] This was the measure by which the Jeffersonians repealed the Federalist lame-duck extension of federal court jurisdiction. See Prologue, above.

course the reason may be merely that, with one or two exceptions,[5] they never had to pass on national measures offensive to Federalist dogma.

That Marshall was a nationalist is familiar, but the mercantile quality of his nationalism is commonly overlooked. In its negative aspects European mercantilism was a weapon against feudal localism. Excepting *Marbury* v. *Madison,* all of the classic decisions of Marshall's Court were thrusts against States-rights localism. Like the feudal system in Europe, state government in Marshall's day was the *bête noire* of commercial interests. Max Lerner has suggested that Marshall found a new way to achieve his party's goals: the common man, who rebelled at Federalist plutocratic theory, was amenable after the War of 1812 to the same interests if clothed in the rhetoric of patriotic nationalism. "It was a crucial discovery," we are told, "and Marshall made the most of it on the judicial front. . . ."[6] This instrumentalist explanation of Marshall's nationalism finds further support in his sympathetic connections with the New England secessionists apropos "Mr. Madison's War."[7]

By what has been called "esoteric statutory construction" in *Brown* v. *Maryland,*[8] Marshall interpreted a national tariff as not merely a revenue or protective measure, but also as a "license" to importers to sell imports (in their "original packages"). Accordingly, by virtue of the Supremacy Clause in Article VI, Sec. 2 of the Constitution, a state tax on importers must give way before this paramount federal "license." Similarly, in *Gibbons* v. *Ogden*[9] he construed the National Coasting License Act to give not merely a competitive advantage to American as against foreign shippers, but also a right of free transit in navigable waters. This federal right, of course, superseded New York's power to encourage the development of steam navigation by giving its inventor a patent,

[5] The most notable exception was the Repeal Act of 1802, which Marshall and his colleagues privately thought unconstitutional but "had not the courage" to invalidate when it came before them in *Stuart* v. *Laird,* 1 Cranch 299 (1803). Beveridge, Albert J., *The Life of John Marshall* (Boston, Houghton Mifflin, 1916–1919), Vol. 3, p. 122.

[6] "John Marshall and the Campaign of History," 39 *Columbia Law Review* 396, 401 (1939).

[7] Beveridge, *op. cit.,* Vol. 4, Chap. 1.

[8] 12 Wheaton 419 (1827).

[9] 9 Wheaton 1 (1824).

i.e., exclusive steamboat rights on the Hudson River for a limited term of years.

In short, "with painful ingenuity" Marshall stretched national legislation to distorted proportions and then applied the principle of national supremacy to limit both the tax and the police powers of the states. But this did not suffice. In each case he went further and suggested—though he seems at pains not to have held—that the state measures would have been invalid even in the absence of national legislation. In this view, the dormant or unexercised Commerce Clause itself constituted a denial of state power. This proposition, taken in conjunction with the extremely broad interpretation of the national commerce power in *Gibbons* v. *Ogden*, was the ultimate in nationalism. For in the case just mentioned, Congress' power to "regulate commerce among the several states" was construed as more than mere authority to deal with traffic or merchandising across state lines. It was power to "govern" all "intercourse" that "concerns [affects] more states than one."

What the Court *held* was highly nationalistic, but it left Congress free to withdraw the federal "licenses" and thus permit the states to tax and regulate. It also showed Congress how to preempt large areas and so insulate them from state control. But what Marshall *suggested* was much more extreme. This would, by virtue of the Constitution itself, exclude the states automatically and permanently from the whole domain of interstate and foreign commerce. Thus no matter how local, how minor, or how important to its welfare, no state would ever touch any incident of the broadly conceived field of national commerce. Why Marshall refrained from holding what he so boldly hinted is a classic riddle. Could he not carry the Court so far? Did he fear Jeffersonian reprisal? Were these trial balloons? Was Marshall himself unsure of his doctrine? We only know that later in a minor opinion Marshall's Court sustained the power of a state to protect health and property from marshland conditions by damming a small, but navigable stream.[10] Though the dam cut off all interstate and foreign intercourse, the opinion simply ignored the earlier suggestion that such matters were the exclusive domain of national authority. It also passed over the fact that the plaintiff held a National Coasting Act license—which according to *Gibbons* v. *Ogden* conferred a right of transit

[10] *Willson* v. *Blackbird Marsh Creek Co.*, 2 Peters 245 (1829).

on navigable water free of state regulation. Presumably the insignificance of the stream in the later case explains the decision.

In these cases Marshall's nationalism is essentially negative: a device for blocking state authority. What of its positive quality? To what extent was Marshall prepared to sustain affirmative national action? Here, too, the opinions have a plain mercantile caste. In *Brown* v. *Maryland* the Court went out of its way to constitutionalize the national tariff. This was the answer to Jefferson's laissez-faire. Similarly, *McCulloch* v. *Maryland* [11] became the occasion for a surprisingly elaborate vindication of the mercantile position in the National Bank controversy. These two opinions are constitutional glosses to Hamilton's *Report on Manufactures, Report on the Public Credit* and related state papers—the classic expressions of Federalist mercantile policy. Indeed, the *McCulloch opinion* is largely a repetition of Hamilton's earlier defense of the bank.[12]

It is one thing for the national government to give tariff and banking aid to private enterprise; to *regulate* business for protection of labor and consumer is something quite different. Such measures Marshall's Court did not have to face. That would come later, after business had grown too big for effective state regulation. Meanwhile, what of Marshall's attitude toward *state* regulation of *local* enterprise and property? In the early days, land speculation was perhaps the major road to riches for those with capital to venture. Marshall, like many of the Founding Fathers, was deeply involved in it. The first case in which the Supreme Court struck down a state measure grew out of a malodorous bit of private enterprise in public land. A northern syndicate bribed most members of the Georgia legislature and so procured 35 million acres of public domain at about a cent and a half an acre. This they resold at an enormous profit. The people of Georgia immediately discovered the Yazoo land fraud and elected a new legislature that repealed the tainted transaction. Those who had purchased from the syndicate hired Hamilton as legal counsel and on his advice initiated *Fletcher* v. *Peck*.[13] Speaking for the Court, Marshall found

[11] 4 Wheaton 316 (1818).

[12] *The Works of Alexander Hamilton,* H. C. Lodge, ed. (New York, Putnam, 1904), Vol. 3. pp. 445–458.

[13] 6 Cranch 87 (1810).

the rescinding act invalid. The Contract Clause (Article I, Sec. 10) with some help from "general principles . . . common to our free institutions" prevented a state from interfering with vested property interests—even those predicated in fraud.

Similarly, in *Dartmouth College* v. *Woodward* [14] New Hampshire was denied power to alter the terms of an old royal charter to make it more amenable to new-world needs. In Jefferson's view, this meant that "the earth belongs to the dead not to the living." The original charter of 1769 had created a self-perpetuating board of trustees to use privately donated funds for educating and Christianizing Indians. By 1815 no Indians were available, and the college community divided politically and religiously on how to operate the school. After a bitter state-wide campaign, the Jeffersonian view prevailed. Legislation was adopted in effect making Dartmouth a state university. The Supreme Court held that in thus abrogating the king's "contract" of 1769, the people of New Hampshire had violated the Contract Clause of the Constitution. Possibly Marshall and his sympathizers were not so much interested in little Dartmouth, as in establishing a precedent for the immunity of business-corporation charters from state control. This, in any case, was the major effect of the decision. Such use of the Contract Clause, designed to prevent states from easing the burdens of debtors via "stay laws" and related measures, seems plainly excessive. Even Marshall seems to have suspected this. In *Dartmouth* he acknowledged that such a case was "not in the mind of the Convention" when it adopted the Contract Clause. Still less must it have been contemplated by those who voted for ratification. In *Fletcher* v. *Peck*, it will be recalled, Marshall felt compelled to buttress his position with "general principles." Apparently when "the great Chief Justice" found the Constitution wanting, he was not above resorting to "natural law" to save commercial ventures from the "evils of democracy."

Conservative tradition insists that by putting the sanctity of "contracts" above other considerations of ethics and public welfare, Marshall and his associates promoted economic stability. Would it not be more accurate to suggest rather that they encouraged the flagrant corruption of state politics and reckless waste of natural

[14] 4 Wheaton 518 (1819).

resources that marked the nineteenth century? Surely judicial protection of fraud in the Yazoo land scandal paved the way for the Robber Barons and their Great Barbecue at the expense of the American people.

Fletcher v. *Peck* and *Dartmouth* are the foundation of what has been called the first doctrine of American constitutional law: the doctrine of vested interests. They are obviously glosses to Blackstone's old-world dicta: "so great is the regard of the law for private property, that it will not authorize the least violation of it; no not even for the general good of the whole community." [15] That Marshall achieved the protection of business interests via the concept of contract is a fascinating gloss to Maine's famous quip on the transition from status to contract as the essence of progress from medieval to modern values.

Blackstone's *Commentaries* were first published in America in 1772. One of the original subscribers was Marshall's father, "who saw to it that his son read Blackstone as carefully as circumstances permitted. He had bought the book for John's use. . . ." [16] Jefferson, like Bentham, hated all that the *Commentaries* stood for. At the newly founded University of Virginia, Blackstone was not to be perpetuated.

> Before the Revolution, Coke on Littleton was the universal elementary book of law for students, and a sounder Whig never wrote, nor of profounder learning . . . in what we called English liberties. . . . [O]ur lawyers then were all Whigs. But when this black-letter text, and uncouth but cunning learning got out of fashion, and the honeyed Mansfieldism of Blackstone became the students' hornbook, from that moment the profession (the nursery of our Congress) began to slide into toryism and nearly all of the young brood of lawyers are now of that hue. They suppose themselves to be Whigs, because they no longer know what Whigism or republicanism means. It is in our seminary [the University of Virginia] that that vestal flame is to be kept alive.[17]

Professor Commager has collected from Jefferson's letters his running commentaries on Marshall's centralizing opinions. The

[15] *Commentaries on the Laws of England,* W. C. Jones, ed. (San Francisco, Bancroft Whitney, 1916), Vol. 1, p. 240.

[16] Beveridge, *op. cit.,* Vol. 1, p. 56.

[17] *The Writings of Thomas Jefferson,* A. E. Bergh, ed. (Washington, D.C., 1907), Vol. 16, p. 156.

Court, said Jefferson,[18] is "the great object of my fear. . . . That body like gravity, ever acting, with noiseless foot, and unalarming advance, gaining ground step by step and holding what it gains, is ingulfing insidiously the special [i.e., state] governments into the jaws of that which feeds them." It is "the subtle corps of sappers and miners constantly working to undermine the foundations of our confederated fabric:" it is "an irresponsible body, working like gravity by night and by day . . . advancing its noiseless step like a thief." It was "setting itself in opposition to the common sense of the nation," "usurping legislation . . . practicing on the Constitution by inferences, analogies and sophisms," "bidding defiance to the whole nation," making the Constitution "a mere thing of wax which they may twist and shape into any form they please."

We have noted Marshall's great concern for national vis-a-vis local interests, and for vested private, as against public, interests. What would his position be when the two preferred claims ran into one another? This essentially is the case of *Gibbons* v. *Ogden*. There a tremendously valuable business "right" based on state law imposed a substantial burden upon national commerce. Marshall and his Court subsumed the former to the latter. This is a striking contrast to *Dartmouth* in which a vested interest prevailed over the public stake in education, and *Fletcher* in which tainted private claims defeated a public proprietary interest. Had Marshall lost his hold upon the Court? Was the steamboat "monopoly" too unpopular to be sustained? Was it merely that *Gibbons* v. *Ogden* subsumed a lesser to a greater commercial interest? Or is it that the independent judiciary, but not a popular legislature, may be trusted to decide when a private right must give way to the public welfare?

One final comment on Marshall's technique. *Brown* v. *Maryland* involved a highly selective license tax on importers. As the Court recognized, its economic effect—if not its linguistic form—brought it within the constitutional prohibition upon state import taxes (Article I, Sec. 10). But that did not suffice. Marshall found it invalid also under the Commerce Clause. Doing so, and ignoring as he did the selective or discriminatory nature of the tax in question, gave the decision a far broader sweep—for interstate

[18] This and the following quotations will be found in Henry S. Commager, *Majority Rule and Minority Rights* (New York, Oxford U.P., 1943), pp. 37–8.

commerce purposes—than was necessary to dispose of the case at issue. Similarly in *Gibbons* v. *Ogden* Marshall chose not to rest decision on the fact that the Constitution gives the patent power to Congress (Article I, Sec. 8). Treating the case rather as a commerce problem enabled him to get far more out of it. Again the effect was to minimize state authority in the commercial area. Obviously the Chief Justice, like other Federalists, had been deeply marked by the experience with state trade barriers under the Articles of Confederation.

It was Marshall's lot to carry on from the bench the program that Hamilton had mapped out as the brains of Washington's administration. The Chief Justice's techniques were novel of necessity. He created them with true genius largely of whole cloth. But the end which his talents served was an anachronism. In the age of Jeffersonian laissez-faire and agrarian States' rights, his opinions vindicated mercantilism and subsumed the claims of democracy to vested business interests. Most of Marshall's classic opinions fall in one or both of these categories. He used national Commerce Clause measures to defeat state power with respect to interstate and foreign matters. He used the Contract Clause to block local authority in local affairs. Excepting only *Gibbons* v. *Ogden* which destroyed the hated steamboat "monopoly," all of his important pronouncements were highly unpopular in their day.[19] But even for the exception Marshall does not deserve unstinted credit. Most of the danger of the steamboat "patent" grew out of *Fletcher* v. *Peck* which placed such legislative grants beyond subsequent legislative control. New York had long wanted to repeal the steamboat grant, but one investigating committee after another reported that to do so would be unconstitutional.[20]

The admiring Beveridge points out that "The conclusion of [Marshall's] early manhood—reluctantly avowed after Washington . . . had bitterly expressed the same opinion, that the people, left to themselves, are not capable of self-government—had [in his mature years] become a profound moral belief." [21] How could one

[19] Beveridge, *op. cit.*, Vol. 4, p. 445; Charles Warren, *The Supreme Court in United States History* (Boston, Little Brown, 1937), Vol. 2, pp. 611 *et. seq.*

[20] See Wallace Mendelson, "New Light on *Fletcher* v. *Peck* and *Gibbons* v. *Ogden*," 58 Yale Law Journal 567 (1949).

[21] *Ibid.*, Vol. 4, p. 488.

who was so out of tune with American ideals as to hate democracy and consider Thomas Jefferson an "absolute terrorist" [22] become a folk-hero? If, as suggested, Marshall's effort tended to perpetuate decadent, old-world ideals in the new land of liberty, how does his popular repute as a great judge survive? For one thing, Marshall's majestic prose, his premise-obscuring rhetoric and inspired generalizations tend to hide the shabby side of the claims which his great opinions protected. More important, Marshall served well the conservative interests of his day—and for a long while it was conservatives who wrote history books. Generations of eulogy by the comfortable classes have left their mark. Few have ventured, as did Holmes, to speak slightingly of Marshall, and that Boston Brahmin almost sacrificed elevation to the highest court of the land for doing it.[23]

Far more, however, is involved than a majestic style or snowballing reverence. What defied the aspirations of the common man in a sparsely settled, agrarian economy has become indispensable to his welfare in a closely integrated industrial economy. Specialization and the division of labor have bound us all together in a tight web of economic interdependence. Our world has so changed in the past sixty or eighty years that Marshall's nationalism, stripped of its immediate mercantile implications, has come of age. (His contract cases are long since dead.) Having built Marshall up so high for so long, conservatives apparently have no stomach now for attacking him. Others have no need to do so. Quite the contrary! Virtually all liberal reform measures of the national government during the past two or three generations are based on visions of national authority adumbrated by Marshall's rhetoric—particularly in *Gibbons* v. *Ogden* and *McCulloch* v. *Maryland.* What was good strategy for early nineteenth century conservatism has become good strategy for mid-twentieth century liberalism. In the days before popular political parties, when businessmen dominated the federal government, they were ardent nationalists. This was a device for defeating state government when it was peculiarly re-

22 For a more extended appraisal see letter to Hamilton quoted in Warren, *op. cit.*, Vol. 1, pp. 183–184.

23 See Oliver W. Holmes, Jr., *Collected Legal Papers* (New York, Harcourt, Brace, 1920), p. 226; and "Oliver Wendell Holmes," Dictionary of American Biography XXI, Supp. 1, 417, 422 (New York, Scribner, 1944).

sponsive to the needs of the common man. It also served to channel gold into business coffers via tariffs, national banks, special trading privileges and related bounties. Thanks to Jeffersonian ideals and innovations in governmental machinery, the federal government is now peculiarly responsive to the aspirations of the common man. It is also the only level of authority competent to meet most of his needs.[24] Accordingly, many business spokesmen have now discovered the special virtues of States' rights—mainly, of course, as a negative upon national authority. On its positive side, the new regard for state authority is as exclusively bounty-minded [25] as was the old nationalism.

[24] A part of the story of state inadequacy is told in the Report of President Eisenhower's Commission on Intergovernmental Relations (1955).

[25] Cf. the tidelands oil controversy.

III

CHIEF JUSTICE TANEY

Jacksonian Democracy

The old-world ideal of government by the "rich and the well-born" died with the Federalist Party early in the nineteenth century. It died, that is, as a publicly avowable program. But what Hamiltonians could no longer do openly they accomplished in effect under the patriotic furor that accompanied the War of 1812. In this era even Calhoun was a thoroughgoing nationalist.

> For better or worse the American masses, and in particular the nationalistic West, had espoused the principle of democracy, and interpreted it in terms of political equalitarianism—a principle that had inspired a fanatical hatred in the breasts of the old Federalists. To gentlemen of that earlier school democracy had meant the right of the propertyless majority to plunder the minority in the name of the law. The later Whigs [successors of the Federalists] did not make so blundering a mistake. Instead of proclaiming democracy the mother of all mischiefs, they welcomed it as an effective aid in vote-getting. Learning their lesson from Jackson, the Whig politicians outdid him in democratic profusions. They had discovered that business had little to fear from a skillfully guided electorate; that quite the safest way, indeed, to reach into the public purse is to do it in the sacred name of the majority will.[1]

Thus Henry Clay refurbished Federalism, replacing Hamilton's dry logic and outspoken contempt for democracy with the glamour of an expanding national self-consciousness. Under a patriotic sugar-

[1] Vernon L. Parrington, *Main Currents in American Thought* (New York, Harcourt, Brace, 1927), Vol. 2, pp. 151–2.

coating Webster and Clay gradually led a "rebaptized Federalism" through Congress and the White House, effectively undoing the accomplishments of the Jeffersonian revolution. The "era of good feeling" meant simply that Hamiltonianism had run up new colors and brought its old cargo—national debt, bank, tariff and internal improvements—safely into port. These measures

dove-tailed neatly in a compact system, based in large part on the debt created by Hamilton's funding plan. The debt made the Bank indispensable as a financial agent, and the tariff indispensable as a source of revenue. The internal-improvements policy promised a future of steady spending which would save the debt from extinction. And the debt itself, by its very existence, bound the government to its creditors, the business and financial groups. "A national debt," said Hamilton, "if it is not excessive, will be to us a national blessing." [2]

This Whiggish mercantile paternalism which deemed the state a mere handmaiden of business interests produced the Jacksonian —as it had earlier the Jeffersonian—outburst. Both were essentially agrarian-labor protests against centralized government of, by, and for the business classes. Jackson and his followers were not levelers. They did not attack business enterprise as such. What they sought was elimination of government-created economic privilege for a select few. Thorough patriots, they saw through Clay's "American system" to its Hamiltonian, mercantile core. "I am one of those," Old Hickory proclaimed, "who do not believe a national debt is a national blessing, but rather a curse to a republic; inasmuch as it is calculated to raise around the administration a moneyed aristocracy dangerous to the liberties of the country." [3] His regime proceeded to extinguish the debt as rapidly as possible.

As for the tariff and its relation to internal improvements, President Jackson observed in his Farewell Address,[4]

Many powerful interests are continually at work to produce heavy duties on commerce and to swell the revenue beyond the real necessities

[2] Arthur Schlesinger, Jr., *The Age of Jackson* (Boston, Little Brown, 1946), p. 11; *The Works of Alexander Hamilton,* H. C. Lodge, ed. (New York, Putnam, 1904), Vol. 3, p. 387

[3] Quoted in Parrington, *op. cit.,* Vol. 2, p. 148.

[4] *A Compilation of the Messages and Papers of the Presidents,* J. D. Richardson, ed. (Washington, 1896). Vol. 3, pp. 292, 299.

of the public service. . . . They succeeded in obtaining a tariff of duties bearing most oppressively on the agricultural and laboring classes of society and producing a revenue that could not be usefully employed within the range of the powers conferred upon Congress, and in order to fasten upon the people this unjust and unequal system of taxation, extravagant schemes of internal improvement were got up in various quarters to squander the money and purchase support. Thus one unconstitutional measure was intended to be upheld by another, and the abuse of the power of taxation was to be maintained by usurping the power of expending the money in internal improvements.

President Jackson's attack upon the Bank has been called "perhaps the most courageous act in our political history." It was one of the first great blows—to be repeated time after time in the unfolding American dream—against intrenched economic privilege. Vetoing the Bank Bill, "Old Hickory" observed,[5]

It is to be regretted that the rich and powerful too often bend the acts of government to their selfish purposes. Distinctions in society will always exist under every government. Equality of talents, of education, or of wealth cannot be produced by human institutions. In the full enjoyment of the gifts of heaven and the fruits of superior industry, economy, and virtue, every man is equally entitled to protection by law; but when the laws undertake to add to these natural and just advantages artificial distinctions, to grant titles, gratuities, and exclusive privileges, to make the rich richer and the potent more powerful, the humble members of society—the farmers, mechanics, and laborers—who have neither the time nor the means of securing like favors to themselves, have a right to complain of the injustice of their government. . . . If we cannot at once, in justice to interests vested under improvident legislation, make our government what it ought to be, we can at least take a stand against all new grants of monopolies and exclusive privileges, against any prostitution of our Government to the advancement of the few at the expense of the many, and in favor of compromise and gradual reform in our code of laws and system of political economy.

But in rejecting mercantile nationalism, the Jacksonians did not countenance disunion or even "confederation." Believing in freedom for the states, they never questioned national sovereignty—as the Carolinian nullifiers quickly discovered. Calhoun made a blundering mistake when he mistook the antimercantilism of the

[5] *Ibid.*, Vol. 2, pp. 576, 590.

old patriot in the White House for susceptibility to *A Disquisition on Government.* Jackson's angry response echoes down through the years, "Our Federal Union—it must and shall be preserved." Of course, the Jacksonians believed in States' rights. But for them this was largely an economic, rather than a political concept. It was not a repudiation of nationalism, but of "the jobbery and corruption and consolidation" towards which Hamilton's and Clay's centralizing, economic paternalism seemed to lead. In a word, the Age of Jackson stood for *genuine* laissez-faire: free play for the equalitarian individualism of an essentially agrarian social order. Because under Federalist and Whig leadership the central government had been the great offender against laissez-faire, the Jacksonians stressed States' rights. This was their weapon against mercantilism, not against the sovereignty of the Union or the supremacy of federal law. Nationalism had been burned into the soul of the leader of the Jacksonians by a British sabre stroke that he received in the Revolution and repaid at the Battle of New Orleans.

While the Jacksonians rejected mercantilism, they had no trace of a leveling, or antibusiness bias. They followed Jefferson in everything except his ideal of an exclusively agrarian paradise. Industrialization had already gone too far for that. Recognizing the trend of the times, Jackson and his followers accepted the business way of life and housebroke it to democracy. This, along with manhood suffrage and abolition of imprisonment for debt, was their great contribution to the Jeffersonian tradition. Business became an interest of the common man, in contrast to the Federalist ideal of a commercial aristocracy. This is symbolized in the move for incorporation by general law to replace the old system of granting corporate charters by special—or private—legislation. The new system made the privilege of incorporation available to all on equal terms. It freed the concept of the corporation from the otherwise inevitable link with monopoly and special privilege. For under the old device of incorporation by special act only the influential could enjoy the corporate way of doing business.

Drawing heavily upon John Taylor of Caroline as official philosopher of Jeffersonianism, Professor Parkes has deftly outlined the essence of the democratic position in the days of Jefferson and Jackson. It upheld the rights of private property, believing that without it there could be no personal freedom; but what it defended was the property which was honestly gained [according to Locke] by the "mixing" of labor with nature, not that acquired by speculation, legal manipulation, or political influence. It sought to create a social system in which all men owned property, or could hope to acquire it, and in which there could be none of the "accumulation of wealth by law without industry" that [was] the essence of aristocracy. It placed no limits on the property any individual could acquire by his own industry, ability and initiative; but it opposed all forms of vested interest and special privilege, and it urged that charters, contracts, and laws of inheritance were made by society and could be changed when their effect was to perpetuate unjust inequalities. It believed, moreover, that given an equitable legal and financial system, which did not protect monopolies or facilitate speculation, then the proper regulator of the economy was the free market, and that the real effect of any political interference with the market [e.g., a tariff] was to create special privileges and to transfer property from those who had rightfully earned it.[6]

Indeed, as Taylor saw it, the whole meaning of Hamiltonianism, as brought up to date by Clay, was to create a capitalist aristocracy of "patronage and paper." This new aristocracy, he thought, was comparable to, but more subtle than, the old feudal variety. It filched wealth created by the labor of the mass of the people, not openly and directly in the manner of feudalism, but by the more complex devices of the mercantile system. Moreover, the new aristocracy

could secure grants of Western land from the government, with the right to collect rents [or mortgage interest] from the farmers who were "mixing their labor" with it; they could acquire farm mortgages by lending money to farmers, and could deprive the farmers of their land if the debts were not repaid; and they could obtain [special charter privileges, giving virtually monopolistic rights—for example in roads, bridges and banks]. Property rights of this kind came under the general heading of contracts. When the richer classes spoke of the protection of property rights as one of the chief functions of government, what they meant was that the government must maintain the sanctity of contracts. . . .

The difference between the property that had originated in the mixing of human labor with the wilderness and the property that had

[6] Henry B. Parkes, *The American Experience* (New York, Knopf, 1955), p. 108.

been acquired by means of a contract was never sharply defined. It was, in fact, impossible to draw any clear line of demarcation between these two forms of property. Yet this difference is the clue to much of the political controversy of eighteenth- and nineteenth-century America.[7]

Judicial decisions, as Max Lerner put it, are not brought by constitutional storks. Indeed the function of law and its minions is to vindicate dominant social ideas, interests and institutions. Thus it is no more surprising that Chief Justice Taney and his associates on the bench should reflect the age of Jackson than that Marshall's Court should have reflected the era of Hamilton. It is noteworthy that both Chief Justices had held high political offices. They had, indeed, been prime movers in the respective regimes which their jurisprudence later implemented. The judicial differences implicit in their divergent politico-economic philosophies were not hidden from competent contemporary observers. The great old Federalist, Chancellor Kent, thought that Taney's Court had "surrendered up to the spirit of the day, the true principles of the Constitution." [8] Marshall's *alter ego*, Mr. Justice Story, considered himself "the last of the old race of judges," [9] as no doubt did Mr. Justice McReynolds a hundred years later. For Daniel Webster the Court was "gone . . . and almost everything is gone or seems rapidly going." [10] The *New York Review* anticipated the sentiments of the Liberty League by a century in complaining, "When we consider the revolution in opinion, in policy and in numbers that has recently changed the character of the Supreme Court, we can scarcely avoid being reduced nearly to a state of despair of the commonwealth." [11] All of this meant merely that the revolutionary waves of 1800 and 1828 had finally in 1837 engulfed the Supreme Court of the United States. Small things sometimes have trenchant symbolic meaning. Like Jefferson, who as President discarded English court apparel and presided over the nation in common American dress, Taney was the first Chief Justice to deliver an opinion in trousers, rather than courtly knee breeches.

[7] *Ibid.*, pp. 343–4.

[8] Reproduced in William W. Story, *Life and Letters of Joseph Story* (Boston, 1851), Vol. 2, p. 270.

[9] *Ibid.*, Vol. 2, p. 277.

[10] Claude H. Van Tyne, *The Letters of Daniel Webster* (New York, McClure Philips, 1902), p. 198.

[11] *New York Review*, Vol. 2, (April 1838), p. 402.

Roger Taney's background was that of a Southern gentleman. During the early part of his mature life he had been an active member of the Federalist Party and had had a substantial commercial law practice. But somewhere along the line what began perhaps as a gentleman's disdain for trade [reinforced possibly by experiences in tobacco markets and by what he saw as counsel and director of the Union Bank of Maryland] developed into a deep skepticism. By 1825, at the age of forty-eight, he was urging the election of Andrew Jackson. Six years later he became Attorney General of the United States, one of President Jackson's most trusted advisers, and spearhead of the fateful attack upon the Bank of the United States.

Taney, of course, wrote a good part of the presidential public papers, particularly the Bank Bill Veto and the Farewell Address, portions of which we have already seen. These and his own public utterances disclose the turn of his mature mind:

> In every period of the world, and in every nation, history is full of examples of combinations among a *few* individuals, to grasp all power in their own hands, and wrest it from the hands of the many. . . . Now for the first time the issue is made up, and the question boldly and distinctly presented to us, whether this noble country is to be governed by the power of money in the hands of the few, or by the free and unbought suffrages of a majority of the people.[12]
>
> It is a fixed principle of our political institutions, to guard against the unnecessary accumulation of power over persons and property in any hands; and no hands are less worthy to be trusted with it than those of a moneyed corporation.[13]

These animadversions against economic privilege and a corresponding faith in the democratic processes are a key to the understanding of Chief Justice Taney and his Court. Perhaps ultimately Marshall's chief contribution was the principle of vigorous judicial intrusion upon the political processes. This followed inevitably from the Federalist premise of distrust for democracy. Jacksonian respect for popular government finds expression in Taney's chief legacy—the concept of judicial self-restraint. Speaking for his

[12] *Daily Albany Argus*, August 29, 1834.

[13] From Taney's *Report from the Secretary of the Treasury on the Removal of the Public Deposits from the Bank of the United States*, Sen. Doc. No. 2, 23rd Cong., 1st Sess., vol. I, p. 20 (1833).

Court in landmark cases, Taney laid down basic boundaries between justiciable and nonjusticiable controversies.[14] The full flavor of his respect for the democratic processes, however, is more plainly illustrated in cases of a less technical nature. *Pennsylvania* v. *The Wheeling and Belmont Bridge Co.*[15] involved Virginia legislation authorizing a bridge across the Ohio River. Pennsylvania, seeking to "protect" its railway and canal system from competition, obtained a Supreme Court order for the removal or modification of the bridge, on the ground that the Virginia authorization conflicted with an act of Congress. The Chief Justice, dissenting, found no relevant national legislation and would leave the matter for Congressional settlement. For him the issues involved—rivalry of two great cities, Pittsburgh and Wheeling, for "commercial headship" of the Ohio River, the conflicting claims of river and railroad in the national economy, the clash between vested interests and technological progress—were essentially legislative in nature. The old rules of the English High Court of Chancery, which a majority purported to be following, were not relevant: [16]

> In taking jurisdiction as the law now stands, we must exercise a broad and undefinable discretion, without any certain and safe rule to guide. . . . [S]uch a discretion appears to me more appropriately to belong to the Legislature than to the Judiciary.
>
> [Congress] has better means . . . of obtaining information, than the narrow scope of judicial proceedings can afford. It may adopt regulations by which Courts of justice may be guided in an inquiry like this with some degree of certainty, instead of leaving them to the undefined discretion which must now be exercised in every case that may be brought before us, without being able to lay down any certain rule, by which this discretion is limited. It is too near the confines of legislation; and I think the Court ought not to assume it.

Taney's position was vindicated in one of those rare instances in which a decision of the Supreme Court was in effect overruled by Congress with the Court's own immediate acquiescence.[17] If a majority of the Justices did not at once perceive the broad policy-

[14] *Lord* v. *Veazie,* 8 Howard 251 (1850); *U.S.* v. *Ferreira,* 13 Howard 40 (1851); *Gordon* v. *U.S.,* 117 U.S. 697 (1865) reported in 1885.

[15] 13 Howard 518 (1852).

[16] *Id.* 587, 592.

[17] *Pennsylvania* v. *Wheeling & Belmont Bridge Co.,* 18 Howard 421 (1856). See also *Milnor* v. *New Jersey Ry.,* 70 U.S. 782, 793, appendix (1857).

determining nature of their original attitude, they were willing to stand corrected by the political branches of government.

Similarly in the famous case of *Luther* v. *Borden* [18] Taney, for the Court, refused to determine which of two rival factions constituted the true government of Rhode Island. That again, being "political" in nature, was not a proper subject for judicial settlement: "Under . . . the Constitution it rests with Congress to decide what government is the established one in a state. . . . And its decision is binding on every other department, and could not be questioned in a judicial tribunal." [19] This is the foundation of the doctrine of political questions which contemplates that courts are not omnicompetent, and that some issues are best resolved by the political processes.

In Taney's day, as in Marshall's, the people still had confidence in the states and looked to them primarily when public action was required. Taney's Court went far in removing the Contract and Commerce Clause impediments that Marshall had imposed upon state authority. The *Charles River Bridge* case,[20] for example, mitigates the doctrine of contractual vested rights. In 1785, when Boston and Charlestown were small towns facing each other on opposite sides of the Charles River, Massachusetts had granted a private company the right to operate an inter-city toll bridge. As the communities grew, the toll rights increased in value and a single bridge became inadequate for the growing traffic. When the state authorized another—competing—bridge in 1828, the owners of the original facility objected on Contract Clause grounds. Taney's opinion for the Court had been foreshadowed in the Bank Bill Veto Message: "If we cannot at once in justice to interests vested under improvident legislation, make government what it ought to be, we can at least take a stand against all new grants of monopolies and exclusive privileges." [21] Translated into judicial principle this became the doctrine of strict construction of legislative grants: [22]

[18] 7 Howard 1 (1849).

[19] *Id.* 42. See also *Kentucky* v. *Dennison,* 24 Howard 66 (1861); *Rhode Island* v. *Massachusetts,* 12 Peters 657, 752 (1838) and 4 Howard 591, 639 (1846); *Kennett* v. *Chambers,* 44 Howard 50 (1852).

[20] 11 Peters 420 (1837).

[21] Richardson, *op. cit.,* Vol. 2, pp. 576, 590.

[22] 11 Peters 420, 549–50 (1837). Cf. the quotation from Franklin, Chap. I at footnote 10, above.

> The whole community are interested in this inquiry, and they have a right to require that the power of promoting their comfort and convenience, and of advancing the public prosperity, by providing safe, convenient, and cheap ways for the transportation of produce and the purposes of travel, shall not be construed to have been surrendered or diminished by the State unless it shall appear by plain words that it was intended to be done. . . . While the rights of property are sacredly guarded, we must not forget, that the community also has rights, and that the happiness and well-being of every citizen depends on their faithful preservation.

Of course, "the last of the old race of judges" was in dissent.[23] "I stand upon the old law," said Story, "upon law established more than three centuries ago . . . in resisting any such encroachments upon the rights and liberties of the citizens, secured by public grant. I will not consent to shake their title deeds by any speculative niceties or novelties." For him time stood still. He was not impressed when the majority observed that if the old bridge charter blocked a new bridge, then old turnpike charters would similarly block canals and railroads. Thus the country would

> be thrown back to the improvements of the last century, and obliged to stand still, until the claims of the old turnpike corporations shall be satisfied; and they shall consent to permit these states to avail themselves of the lights of modern science, and to partake of the benefit of those improvements which are now adding to the wealth and prosperity, and the convenience and comfort, of every part of the civilized world. . . . [I]f such a right of property exists, we have no lights to guide us in marking out its extent, unless, indeed, we resort to the feudal grants, and to the exclusive rights of ferries, by prescription, between towns; and are prepared to decide that when a turnpike road from one town to another has been made, no railroad or canal, between these two points, could afterwards be established.[24]

To protect the public—and new forms of property—by strict construction of public grants is one thing; to deny state power to make binding contracts is something quite different. If a state had *unequivocally* committed itself; if its constitution permitted it to do so; if it had received a *quid pro quo,* and had not destroyed its future power to govern, Jacksonian judges could be counted upon

23 *Ibid.*
24 *Ibid.*

to enforce the agreement.[25] The right of local self-government includes the right to make mistakes, and it is not the function of the federal judiciary to save the states from the consequences of their own bad bargains. Indeed, "the principle that they are the best judges of what is for their own interest, is the foundation of our political institutions." [26] So too, in *Bronson* v. *Kinzie* [27] Taney for the Court vindicated the Contract Clause *in its intended sense* by striking down state moratoria legislation growing out of the depression of 1837. The *Charles River Bridge* and similar cases suggest that Taney was skeptical of Marshall's use of the Contract Clause to cover executed state "contracts," or grants. To use that clause as intended, that is, to protect executory agreements between private parties, was another matter.

Surely in these cases there is no trace of agrarian radicalism, no Procrustean impulse to tailor the nation to the Jeffersonian ideal of a farm Utopia. They limit Marshall's doctrine of vested rights, but do not destroy it. If business is to prosper, men must have assurance that contracts will be enforced. On the other hand, no community could survive without some authority to control agreements that jeopardize the public welfare. On the first proposition Marshall and Taney were in full agreement; on the second they were largely at odds—at least in emphasis. Taney construed the ancient bridge charter strictly to keep it from interfering with important public needs *including the rise of the canal and railroad industries.* As usual the problem was not one of destroying property for some "leveling" purpose, but of balancing older against newer proprietary needs. As Louis Boudin suggests, with perhaps some exagger-

[25] See *Piqua Branch Bank* v. *Knoop,* 16 Howard 369 (1853); *Ohio Life Ins. Co.* v. *Debolt,* 16 Howard 416 (1853); and cf. *River Bridge Co.* v. *Dix,* 6 Howard 507 (1848). Referring to these and the *Charles River Bridge* cases, Professor Borchard has said that Taney was so convinced that "Government may . . . be imposed upon, especially by corporate interests who usually [under the special act system] draw their own charters, that he was averse to any bargaining away of the police power, the power of eminent domain or the taxing power. The burden of proving the derogation from the public right was thrown on the private interest, and while a clear contract for good consideration . . . would be upheld, it had to be made exceptionally clear that the exemption was adequately paid for and that no supervening right of the public was impaired." "Taney's Influence On Constitutional Law," 24 Georgetown Law Journal 848, 853 (1936).

[26] *Ohio Life Ins. Co.* v. *Debolt,* 16 Howard 416, 429 (1853).

[27] 1 Howard 311 (1843).

ation, "The interests of the community are always on the side of new forms of property, while the interests of the possessors of old forms of property are always opposed to the interests of the community." [28] Marshall's doctrine of vested interests plainly favored older as against newer claims.[29] It is not to be forgotten that Marshall lived to hear the *Charles River Bridge* case, though he died before its decision. We know on Mr. Justice Story's authority that the "great Chief Justice" concurred in the dissenting view in that case.[30]

The Contract Clause was only one of the Old Court's weapons against the states. It will be recalled that Marshall also found implicit in the Commerce Clause a severe (or absolute) restraint upon local self-government. Taney himself rejected this completely: [31]

> . . . it appears to me to be very clear, that the mere grant of power to the general government cannot, upon any just principles of construction, be construed to be an absolute prohibition to the exercise of any power over the same subject by the States. The controlling and supreme power over commerce with foreign nations and the several States is undoubtedly conferred upon Congress. Yet, in my judgment, the State may nevertheless . . . make regulations for its own territory; and such regulations are valid unless they come in conflict with a law of Congress.

It followed, of course, that the remedy for undue state interference with national commerce lay in an appeal to Congress and not to the courts, the determination of commercial policy being a legislative, not a judicial, function. In a word, the commerce power had been given to Congress and not to the courts—nor had it been prohibited to the states.[32]

But Marshall had left his mark upon the law. After years of

[28] "John Marshall and Roger B. Taney," 24 Georgetown Law Journal 864, 893 (1936).

[29] A possible exception was *Gibbons* v. *Ogden* discussed in Chap. II, above.

[30] See Story's dissent in the *Charles River Bridge* case.

[31] *The License Cases,* 5 Howard 504, 579 (1847).

[32] Taney did hold that some powers of the national Government were exclusive because of their inherent nature, though, as in the case of the commerce power, they were not expressly denied to the states in the Constitution. *Holmes* v. *Jennison,* 14 Pet. 540 (1840) concerning extradition; *Taylor* v. *Canyl,* 20 How. 583 (1858) concerning maritime jurisdiction.

struggle, a compromise, silently accepted by Taney, became orthodox doctrine:[33]

> . . . [T]he power to regulate commerce, embraces a vast field, containing not only many, but exceedingly various subjects, quite unlike in their nature; some imperatively demanding a single uniform rule . . . and some . . . as imperatively demanding that diversity, which alone can meet the local necessities. . . .

It followed, that with respect to the former, the states could not act at all, whereas with respect to the latter, they were free to govern—in the absence, of course, of conflicting national legislation. In other words, Marshall's idea of exclusive national authority prevailed in the one area, while Taney's concurrent view prevailed in the other. As it turned out, this was more than half a loaf for Taney's position; future cases were to hold that even in the "exclusive area" Congress could authorize state legislation.[34]

It was suggested above that one of the major Jacksonian contributions was the reconciliation of the corporate and the democratic ways of life. Judicial aspects of this are seen in a number of cases. *Bank of Augusta* v. *Earle*[35] overruled an agrarian-inspired lower court decision which would have deprived corporations of capacity to do business outside of the respective states in which they were organized. But in so doing, the Court did not adopt Webster's Whiggish proposition that corporations are citizens within the contemplation of the Privileges and Immunities clause of the Constitution (Article IV, Sec. 2) and so entitled to wander from state to state free from special local regulation. Nowadays it is easy to forget that corporations were once, somewhat like labor unions today, looked upon as "soulless monsters" of dangerous propensity. Reflecting this general distrust, and at the same time appreciating the needs of an expanding industrialism, Taney's Court reversed the decision below and held that corporations have the capacity, but only the capacity and not a constitutional right, to operate outside of their respective incorporating states. Thus while the interests of business were vindicated, so also were those of the community. For under this decision the states retained power through

[33] *Cooley* v. *Bd. of Wardens,* 12 Howard 299, 319 (1851).

[34] *Clark Distilling Co.* v. *Western Md. Ry.*, 242 U.S. 311 (1917); *Prudential Ins. Co.* v. *Benjamin,* 328 U.S. 408 (1946). See Chap. VI, below.

[35] 13 Peters 519 (1839).

their political processes to exclude or regulate out-of-state corporations seeking to do business within their borders—a power analogous, of course, to that which the chartering process gives in regard to domestic corporations.[36] Similarly, *Letson's* case [37] killed an old implication [38] that corporations were not within the diversity jurisdiction of the federal courts. *Swift* v. *Tyson* [39] undertook in the exercise of that jurisdiction to promote a unified, nation-wide, commercial common law for the convenience of business.[40]

The decisions so far considered have emphasized the sanctity of legislative processes and the freedom of the states to handle local problems with a minimum of judicial interference. But it is a false antithesis which, contrasting Marshall and Taney, depicts the latter as an advocate of agrarian particularism. Jackson's forceful repudiation of nullification finds analogous expression in *Ableman* v. *Booth* [41] which upholds the unqualified power of the national Government to enforce national law without state interference. The case of *The Genessee Chief*,[42] greatly expanding the maritime jurisdiction of the central government, hardly bespeaks an invidious States' rights attitude; nor does *Holmes* v. *Jennison*,[43] affirming exclusive federal power over extradition; or *Swift* v. *Tyson*, generating a national, common law for commerce; or *Dobbins* v. *Erie County* [44] denying state authority to tax the pay of federal officials; or *Almy* v. *California* [45] denying state power to tax goods leaving for outside markets; or *Bank of Commerce* v. *New York* [46] restraining state interference with the national borrowing power.

Obviously on occasion Taney's Court could call a halt upon

36 See *Terral* v. *Burke Const. Co.*, 257 U.S. 529 (1922) for the doctrine of unconstitutional conditions; *Western Union* v. *Kansas*, 216 U.S. 1 (1910) for Commerce Clause limitations.

37 *Louisville, C. & C. Rd.* v. *Letson*, 2 Howard 497 (1844).

38 *Bank of U.S.* v. *Deveanx*, 5 Cranch 61 (1808).

39 16 Peters 1 (1842).

40 Presumably the thought behind this decision was that the state courts would follow the lead of the federal judiciary. When they failed to do so, havoc resulted and eventually the principle case was overruled in *Erie RR* v. *Tompkins*, 304 U.S. 64 (1938).

41 21 Howard 506 (1859).

42 12 Howard 443 (1851).

43 14 Peters 540 (1840).

44 16 Peters 435 (1842). This was an extension of *McCulloch* v. *Maryland*.

45 24 Howard 169 (1860).

46 2 Black 620 (1862).

state government. Yet its major theme was the principle of judicial self-restraint. It laid out abiding lines between justiciable and non-justiciable conflicts; it originated the doctrine of political questions; it eased the principles of vested rights and the exclusive commerce power as restraints upon state legislation; it initiated the tradition that in Commerce Clause matters Congress can override the Court as to the scope of state authority; and, finding a place for business corporations in the structure of American law, it refused to immunize them from legislative control as urged by so responsible a Whig lawyer as Daniel Webster. Finally Chief Justice Taney struck the first great blow for civil liberty in federal court history.[47] In a decision which he had every reason to believe—as he wrote his wife—could easily have ended his public career, he repudiated the power of the President and the militia to suspend the writ of habeas corpus and thereby to deny an accused the right of trial by jury. True to his faith in the legislative processes,[48] the great Jacksonian judge held that power to suspend the ancient freedom writ lay only in Congress.

Now the great paradox. In view of his deep Jacksonian respect for popular sovereignty and the democratic way of life, how could Taney towards the end of his career suddenly "blunder" into the *Dred Scott* catastrophe?[49] How could a Court that had so long deferred to the political branches for solution of policy issues have undertaken to decide the most controversial political issue of the day? Early, Abolitionist-inspired vituperation has now given way to general acceptance of *Dred Scott* as an honest judicial effort to settle a nation-wrecking problem.[50] This, no doubt, is accurate, but incomplete. A fuller explanation takes us back many years in the history of one of America's oldest and most persistent problems—whose ghost has not yet been stilled.

Acquisition of the Mexican and Oregon territories in the 1840's had revived the old problem of extension of slavery. The Wilmot Proviso, supported by resolutions of all but one Northern state

[47] *Ex parte Merryman,* 17 Fed. Cas. 144, No. 9487 (C.C.D. Md. 1861). Cf. *Ex parte Bollman,* etc., 4 Cranch 75 (1807).

[48] Cf., for example, Taney's position in the two *Wheeling Bridge Cases* and in *Luther* v. *Borden.*

[49] *Scott* v. *Sanford,* 19 Howard 393 (1857).

[50] See, for example, Charles Evans Hughes, "Roger Brook Taney," 17 A.B.A.J. 785, 787 (1931).

legislature, would have imposed freedom in the new domain by act of Congress. After its adoption by the House of Representatives in 1847, Southern leaders abandoned their willingness to extend the Missouri Compromise and insisted that Congress had no power to prohibit slavery anywhere. On this issue Congress was deadlocked; while the Northern view prevailed in the House, it was blocked in the Senate.

This impasse is the background of the attempted Clayton Compromise [51] of mid-1848, whereby Congress in organizing territorial government was to remain silent on the subject of slavery, leaving its introduction or prohibition to rest

> . . . on the Constitution, as the same should be expounded by the [territorial] judges, with a right to appeal to the Supreme Court of the United States.

In this manner, according to Senator Clayton of Maine, Congress would "avoid the decision of this distracting question, leaving it to be settled by the silent operation of the Constitution itself. . . ." [52] After elaborate debate the Clayton Compromise was passed in the Senate and defeated in the House (the latter still intent upon the Wilmot Proviso). But the essence of Clayton's proposal lived on to be incorporated in the great Compromise of 1850 and the Kansas-Nebraska Act of 1854 and to reach fruition in the *Dred Scott* decision.

The second resolution of Clay's famous 1850 Compromise openly acknowledged the congressional deadlock: ". . . it is inexpedient for Congress to provide by law either for [slavery's] introduction into, or exclusion from, any part of said territory . . . ." [53] Accordingly, the issue of slavery was left to be settled by the Constitution, i.e., by judicial review. When amendments were offered to "clarify" the situation, Clay responded: [54]

> The bill leaves in full force the paramount authority of the Constitution. . . . Now what ought to be done more satisfactory to both sides of the question, to the free States and to the slave-holding States,

[51] Cong. Globe, 30th Cong., 1st Sess. 950, 1002 (1848).
[52] *Ibid.*
[53] Sen. J., 31st Cong. 1st Sess. 118 (1850); Cong. Globe, 31st Cong., 1st Sess. 245 (1850).
[54] *Id.* at 1155.

than to apply the principle of [Congressional] non-intervention to the state of the law [in the territory] and to leave the question of slavery or no slavery to be decided by the only competent authority that can definitely settle it forever, the authority of the Supreme Court of the United States.

The honorable Senator from Connecticut [Mr. Baldwin] on yesterday wanted the law settled. Suppose, then, we were to make a declaration of the law pleasing to the learned Senator . . . how if we were to attempt to settle this question could it be settled? In the first place we can not settle it, because of the great diversity of opinion which exists; and yet the Senator will ask those who differ with him in opinion to surrender their opinion, and, after they have made this sacrifice of opinion, can they declare what the law is? When the question comes up before the Supreme Court of the United States, that tribunal will declare what the law is.

On this basis the slavery extension aspects of the Compromise of 1850 were "settled." Congress simply delegated to the territorial legislatures all power over slavery which Congress itself might have, the extent of that power being the subject of vigorous dispute: [55]

. . . the legislative power of the territory shall extend to all rightful subjects of legislation consistent with the Constitution of the United States [with certain exceptions not here relevant].

Then to facilitate decision of the constiutional question, special liberalizing provisions were made in regard to federal court jurisdiction in slavery litigation. Thus after providing that "writs of error and appeals [to the Supreme Court] from the final decisions of said [territorial] court shall be allowed . . . where the . . . amount in controversy . . . shall exceed one thousand dollars . . . ," special exception was made "in all cases involving title to slaves" where it was provided, "the said writs of error or appeals shall be allowed . . . without regard to the value of the matter . . . in controversy. . . ." Similarly "a writ of error or appeal shall be allowed to the Supreme Court of the United States . . . upon any writ of habeas corpus involving the question of personal freedom. . . ." [56]

These provisions are a verbatim copy of parts of the Clayton

[55] The Texas and New Mexico Act, 9 Stat. 446 (1850); The Utah Act, 9 Stat. 453 (1850).

[56] *Ibid.*

Compromise which had been added to Senator Clayton's original bill after Senators Hamlin and Corwin had raised the point that the normal federal jurisdictional amount of one thousand dollars would prevent effective operation of Clayton's proposal to shunt the slavery extension issue over to the courts.[57] It is, of course, significant that both provisions liberalizing the right of appeal to the Supreme Court—the one relating to habeas corpus as well as that eliminating the "jurisdictional amount"—were new in federal law. Senator Corwin's comment on the scheme is apposite—Congress had enacted a law suit, not a law.

This interpretation was adopted by Senator Stephen A. Douglas' Committee on Territories which reported out on January 4, 1854, the Dodge Bill for the organization of the Nebraska Territory: [58]

> In the judgment of your committee, those measures [the acts constituting the Compromise of 1850] were intended to have a far more comprehensive and enduring effect than the mere adjustment of the difficulties arising out of the recent acquisition of Mexican territory. They were designed to establish certain great principles, which would . . . in all time to come, avoid the perils of a similar agitation, by withdrawing the question of slavery from the halls of Congress and the political arena, and committing it to the arbitrament of those who were immediately interested in, and alone responsible for its consequences. [There follows recital of some of the arguments as to the constitutionality of slavery in the territories and of the power of Congress with respect to slavery.] Your committee do not feel themselves called upon to enter into the discussion of these controverted questions. They involve the same grave issues which produced the agitation, the sectional strife, and the fearful struggle of 1850. As Congress deemed it wise and prudent to refrain from deciding the matters in controversy then . . . by any act declaratory of the true intent of the Constitution . . . so your committee are not now prepared to recommend a departure from the course pursued on that memorable occasion . . . by any act declaratory of the meaning of the Constitution in respect to the legal points in dispute . . . it is apparent that the compromise measures of 1850 affirm and rest upon the following propositions—First: That all questions pertaining to slavery in the territories, and in the new States to be

57 Cong. Globe, 30th Cong., 1st Sess. 988, 989, 1002–5 (1848).
58 Sen. Rep. No. 15, 33rd Cong., 1st Sess. (1854).

formed therefrom, are to be left to the decision of the people residing therein. . . .

Second: That all cases involving title to slaves, and "questions of personal freedom" are referred to the adjudication of the local tribunals, with the right of appeal to the Supreme Court of the United States.

These principles, drawn from the Compromise of 1850, were embedded in the Kansas-Nebraska Act. In the course of the debate thereon Senator Brown gives what Allen Johnson calls the Southern viewpoint: [59]

> If I thought that, in voting for the bill as it now stands, I was conceding the right of the people in the territory, during their territorial existence, to exclude slavery, I would withhold my vote. . . . It [the bill] leaves the question where I am quite willing it should be left—to the ultimate decision of the courts. It is purely a judicial question, and if Congress will refrain from intimating an opinion, I am willing that the Supreme Court shall decide it. But, Sir, I have too often seen that Court sustaining the intentions of Congress, to risk a decision in my favor, after Congress has decided against me. The alien and sedition laws, the bank law, the tariff law have all been decided constitutional. And why? Not, in my opinion, because they were so, but because the Supreme Court, as a coordinate Department of Government, was disinclined to clash with the other Departments. If this question is allowed to go before the Supreme Court, free from the influence of a Congressional prejudgment, I will abide the result though it be against me.

Similar views were expressed by many others from all parts of the country.[60]

Congressmen and Senators were not the only ones who understood that the slavery-extension problem was not to be settled judicially. In a public speech at Galena, Illinois, Abraham Lincoln echoed Senator Brown's position:

> Do you [Democrats] say that such restrictions of slavery [in the territories] would be unconstitutional and that some of the States would not submit to its enforcement? I grant you that an unconstitutional act is not a law; but I do not ask, and will not take your construction of the Constitution. The Supreme Court of the United States is the tribunal

[59] Cong. Globe, 33d Cong., 1st Sess., appendix, 232 (1854); Johnson, *Stephen A. Douglas* (New York, Macmillan, 1908), p. 247.

[60] For a fuller view of this whole matter see Wallace Mendelson, "Dred Scott's Case—Reconsidered," 38 Minnesota Law Review 16 (1953).

to decide such questions, and we [Republicans] will submit to its decisions. . . .[61]

There had been some doubt as to whether President Pierce would sign the Kansas-Nebraska Act, for he had been suspected of free-soilism. To resolve any such doubts, Secretary of War Jefferson Davis arranged a conference between the President and a number of leading Senators and Congressmen, where administration support for the measure was secured. Indeed, as it turned out, the President personally believed the Missouri Compromise unconstitutional, but rather than repeal by the Kansas-Nebraska Act, he favored a "guarantee of rights of persons and property in accordance with the Constitution, and would leave it to the Supreme Court to decide what those rights were."[62] In his last message to Congress on December 22, 1856, President Pierce in effect endorsed the *Dred Scott* decision in advance:[63]

> All that the repeal [of the Missouri Compromise by the Kansas-Nebraska Act] did was to relieve the statute book of an objectionable enactment, unconstitutional in effect and injurious in terms to a large portion of the states.

In his inaugural address two days before the *Dred Scott* decision, President-elect Buchanan, referring to the problem of slavery in the territories, said:[64]

> [I]t is a judicial question, which legitimately belongs to the Supreme Court of the United States before whom it is now pending, and will, it is understood, be speedily and finally settled. . . . The whole Territorial question being thus settled upon the principle of popular sovereignty—a principle as ancient as free government itself—everything of a practical nature has been decided.

Clearly the treatment of slavery in the territories as a judicial question by important political figures on such occasions indicates a rather general public acceptance of that mode of settlement. Similarly in his first public mention of the matter after the *Dred*

[61] July 26, 1856, *The Collected Works of Abraham Lincoln*, R. P. Basler ed. (New Brunswick, Rutgers U.P., 1953), Vol. 2, pp. 354–5.
[62] Henry H. Simms, *A Decade of Sectional Controversy* (Chapel Hill, Univ. of N.C.P., 1942), pp. 59–60.
[63] Richardson, *op. cit.* Vol. 5, p. 403.
[64] *Id.* p. 431.

Scott decision Douglas explained that by the Kansas-Nebraska Act Congressional power over slavery in the territories had been referred to the Supreme Court. The latter having spoken, it was the duty of all good citizens to accept the decision. Indeed, Douglas praised the Court for having passed over mere "technicalities" and turned its decision upon the true merits of the issue.[65]

In the presidential campaign of 1860, Lincoln and Douglas held the positions they had taken in their famous Illinois debates in 1858—the one bitterly rejecting the *Dred Scott* decision, the other supporting it. Breckinridge, nominee of the Southern wing of the Democratic Party, also endorsing the famous decision, demanded its implementation by a Congressional "slave code" for the territories. This was the South's answer to the Douglas Freeport Doctrine. Clay and Douglas had held the nation and the Democratic Party together by a compromise that transferred the most vexing problem of the day from the political to the judicial arena. This entailed an understanding that, win or lose, each claimant would accept the judicial settlement when it should finally come. But the North proved unwilling to do so. The Republicans, notwithstanding Lincoln's Galena pledge, repudiated the *Dred Scott* decision outright. The Northern Democrats, following the "little giant," attempted escape by a legal quibble: the *Dred Scott* case, they held, ruled only upon the question of Congressional power over slavery. Their platform pledged them to await and accept a Supreme Court decision on the power of the territorial legisla-

[65] Speech to the Grand Jury, Springfield, Illinois, June 12, 1857. See George F. Milton, *The Eve of Conflict* (Boston, Houghton Mifflin, 1934) p. 260. It will be noted, of course, that it was Douglas who won the Lincoln-Douglas debates, in the sense that it was he who won the prize at stake, a seat in the United States Senate. In that campaign the meaning and implications of the *Dred Scott* case were thoroughly canvassed by its leading critic and its leading apologist.

Of course the *Dred Scott* case did not arrive at the Supreme Court via the procedural (i.e., jurisdiction-liberalizing) route provided in either the Compromise of 1850 or the Kansas-Nebraska Act, but, as Douglas recognized in the Grand Jury Speech, it did dispose of the substantive issue contemplated by that legislation. Lincoln's recognition of the latter point is implicit in his "House-divided" speech (Springfield, Illinois, June 17, 1858) where he sees a conspiracy between "Stephen [Douglas], Franklin [Pierce], Roger [Taney], and James [Buchanan]"—the main elements of their "plot" being the language of the Kansas-Nebraska Act, the *Dred Scott* decision and the *a priori* endorsements thereof of both Presidents.

tures.[66] Upon the issues so joined, Lincoln received 1,866,452 votes, as against a combined total of 2,226,738 for Douglas and Breckinridge. Lincoln's party obtained only a minority in each house of Congress. This could hardly be called a popular repudiation of the principle of judicial settlement or indeed of the *Dred Scott* decision itself.

Shortly after the election, on the eve of Secession, Senator Crittinden, Clay's successor in the Senate as fate would have it, proposed a settlement which would have written an extended Missouri Compromise into the Constitution. He could not even get it through a Senate Committee. That approach to the slavery problem had not been politically feasible since the impasse of 1846–1850. Resort to war between the states followed not, as some would have it, because political settlement had been foreclosed by judicial action, but more likely because the issues cut too deeply to be solved either by courts or legislatures. The real misfortune of the *Dred Scott* decision was that, duly distorted, it served as a powerful weapon for the Abolitionists—always a small, fanatical minority.

The Court had not intruded upon legislative policy; it had not thwarted the democratic process. Rather Congress, the statesmen of the day, and indeed the people after years of struggle found themselves unable to settle the bitterest issue that America has ever faced. Quite consciously they passed the buck to the Supreme Court. Had the judges rejected it, Father Hopkins insists, posterity would be entitled to ask why the last peaceful means for settlement had not been tried.

[66] Douglas spelled out the constitutional theories behind this position in "The Dividing Line Between Federal and Local Authority, Popular Sovereignty in the Territories," *Harper's New Monthly Magazine*, Vol. 19 (September, 1859), p. 519. His main point was that the territorial legislative power is not derivative but independent of, and broader than, Congressional power in respect to slavery.

IV

MR. JUSTICE FIELD

"Laissez Faire"

War seems to create—or leave unresolved—at least as many problems as it settles. When Charles Francis Adams brought his family home from England after the Civil War, his son, Henry, observed that "Had they been Tyrian traders of the year B.C. 1000, . . . they could hardly have been stranger on the shore of a new world, so changed from what it had been ten years earlier." [1] What impressed them most, according to the senior Adams, was the

> greatly enlarged grasp of [business] enterprise and increased facility of combination. The great operations of war, the handling of large masses of men, the influence of discipline, the lavish expenditure of unprecedented sums of money, the immense financial operations, the possibilities of effective cooperation were lessons [2]

not lost on the business community.

In the forty years following 1859, American coal production grew from 16 to 260 million tons, pig-iron from 800,000 to 14 million tons, railroad trackage from 30,000 to 193,000 miles. In the same period capital invested in manufacturing increased tenfold to $10 billion, finally overtaking that invested in agriculture. The number of industrial workers grew from 1,300,000 to 5,300,000 and

[1] Henry Adams, *The Education of Henry Adams* (Boston, Houghton Mifflin, 1918), p. 237.

[2] Charles H. Adams, "An Erie Raid," *North American Review*, Vol. CXII (April, 1871), p. 241.

the value of industrial produce expanded from $2 billion to more than $13 billion per year. Commercial oil production began in 1859. Within forty years the oil trust had been established. Its creator, John D. Rockefeller, pointed out that "large-scale organization had revolutionized the way of doing business. . . . The time was ripe for it. It had come. . . . The day of combination is here to stay. Individualism has gone, never to return." [3] By 1904 Moody could list 318 "greater" or "lesser" trusts representing a consolidation of 5300 formerly competing plants. By 1912, the Pujo Committee found that J. P. Morgan and his associates held directorships in 112 corporations with total resources of about twenty-two billion dollars. This was more than the total assessed value of all property in the twenty-two states and territories west of the Mississippi River and more than twice the assessed value of all property in the thirteen southern states.

Obviously Jefferson's old dream of an agricultural Utopia would not be fulfilled. By the end of the Civil War, Hamiltonianism was well on the way to total victory. Its new prophet was Andrew Carnegie. As a disillusioned young man in the 1860's, he devoted his life to the acquisition of a business fortune—though he found it "degrading beyond recovery." "This amassing of wealth is one of the worst species of idolatry—no idol is more debasing than the worship of money. . . ." [4] Here was a man of conscience caught up in the materialism of his day and suffering for it. Then, according to his *Autobiography,* he discovered Herbert Spencer and "light came as in a flood and all was clear. . . . I had found the truth of evolution." A conscience inherited from a more generous era was no longer an obstacle. He found a way—for himself and for his age—to reconcile it with the "idolatry" of amassing money. The new faith was The Gospel of Wealth: [5]

> We of the capitalistic persuasion put trust in the individual man. We make him a part, according to his particular skill, of a great and far-reaching industrial organization. We demote him when his ability fails,

[3] Quoted in Allan Nevins, *John D. Rockefeller* (New York, Scribner, 1940), Vol. 1, p. 622.

[4] Reproduced in Burton J. Hendrick, *The Life of Andrew Carnegie* (Garden City, Doubleday Doran, 1932), Vol. 1, p. 147.

[5] Ralph H. Gabriel, *The Course of American Democratic Thought,* 2nd. ed. (New York, Ronald, 1956), p. 163.

and discard him if we find a serious flaw of character. In our system there is nothing, save his own shortcomings, to prevent his rising from the bottom to the top. We have, then, a method, better than that of practical politics, for selecting the leaders of a democracy. By a process of pitiless testing we discover who are the strong and who are the weak. To the strong we give power in the form of the autocratic control of industry and of wealth with which the leader, who has thus risen by a process of natural selection, can and does do for the masses of the community what they could never do for themselves. We agree with Alexander Hamilton that the voice of the able few should be equal to, nay, greater than that of the mediocre many in the actual government of society. So we demand that the political State shall leave us alone. We have little faith in the State as a constructive agency and less in it as an efficient instrument. The politician is a slave to the whims of the masses, a master of favoritism for his own ends, and a waster of the public substance. We demand of the State protection of property. For this purpose we ask an adequate police, a sound banking system, a sound currency based on gold, and court decisions to nullify social legislation confiscatory in character. We demand a tariff to protect us against our foreign competitors and a navy to guard our commerce and our stakes in other lands. When the State has fulfilled these, its proper functions, we ask it to leave us alone. We point to the progress already achieved under *laissez faire*. We guarantee that, if our conditions are met, the sun of prosperity will fill the land with light and happiness.

The effectiveness of a faith or myth, of course, does not depend upon its truth or internal consistency. Few questioned the relevance of biological "natural selection" to the man-made institutions of Hamiltonianism. Only radicals saw incongruity in individualism as a belief vis-a-vis the corporation and trust as a way of life. Only the impertinent questioned the application of frontier ideals to an urban industrial society. But few outsiders wondered how aggressive, individual self-concern could produce social harmony. All this, along with more tangible abuses by the great tycoons, was irrelevant. The crucial thing was that the Gospel of Wealth worked. It inspired generations, and brought economic goods in kind and quantity beyond belief. Buttressed with vast natural resources, and free of old-world social strictures, it all but solved man's oldest problem: shortage of the necessities and amenities of life. If the cost came high in broken lives, perverted traditions, and moral insensitivity, the achievement also was great.

The foundation of Jeffersonian and Jacksonian democracy had been a political alliance between the agrarian West and South, with increasing support from urban workers. When slavery finally broke the Democratic coalition and isolated the South, the Republicans formed a winning combination of West and Northeast. As Wilfred Binkley demonstrates, Lincoln's Republican Party had been mainly an agrarian-labor alliance, but during Grant's administration it was captured by powerful business forces.[6] This gave it incongruous geo-economic wings. To stay in power *politically*, Northern business needed the support of its bitterest *economic* enemy—the Western farmer. A drastic drop in farm commodity prices and abiding agricultural depression after Appomattox contrasted sharply with the business boom. Farmers saw the cause in the very things that their Hamiltonian "allies" found indispensable: "hard" money; tariffs; trusts; regressive taxes; along with extortionate railroad rates and fiscal practices. No wonder the bloody shirt had to be waved so strenuously to sustain the Republician alliance of Big Business and little farmer! This perhaps is why the judiciary became so involved in matters of economic policy in the Republican era. With the South neutralized by an emotional barrier that defied economic expediency, sectional realignment as in 1800 and 1860 was impossible.[7] This left the West and Northeast wedded incompatibly in a union which neither could dominate by ordinary political devices.[8] Yet their differences, i.e., economic policy, had to be settled somehow. *Significantly the crucial economic issues that came before the Supreme Court in the post-bel-*

6 Wilfred E. Binkley, *American Political Parties* (New York, Knopf, 1945), p. 232.

7 In 1800 the Jeffersonians broke the Federalist South-Northeast combination and created the winning coalition of South and West. Lincoln succeeded in 1860 by substituting a Northeast-West alliance for the old West-South combination.

8 This Republican "combination, though strong enough to win the Presidency, did not possess the strength needed to control Congress under normal conditions. Hence, the frantic efforts of the Republican leaders, first to extend their power into the South by means of Negro votes and later to strengthen themselves in the West by the admission of new states and the cultivation of Western interests. . . . But populism ruined Republican hopes in the West as the failure of Negro suffrage ruined them in the South. . . ." Holcombe, "Present-day Characteristics of American Political Parties," in Edward B. Logan, *The American Political Scene* (New York, Harper, 1938), p. 19.

lum era were clashes of interest between grain farmer and businessman—the major "partners" in the dominant political party. Here was an entree for judicial policy-making on a grand scale.[9] Would the Court serve as mediator between the hostile wings of the Republican Party? Would it undertake, that is, to fill the political vacuum resulting from ossification of sectional politics? To do so would make it the "final" arbiter of economic policy.

When Morrison B. Waite became Chief Justice in 1874, the legal problems of the war itself had been largely settled. But legislation growing out of tensions provoked by the industrial revolution raised new "legal" issues. How far could the community go in subjecting private business to public control? To meet this problem two traditions were available: Taney's Judicial Tolerance, which assumed that social conflicts in a democracy are best solved by the political processes; and Marshall's Judicial Supremacy, which seemed to suppose that ultimately only the judiciary "can be assumed to have capacity to govern." Both traditions were strongly represented on Waite's Court: the former by the Chief Justice himself, the latter by the forceful Mr. Justice Field. Between these two, the future hung poised as at no other time in our judicial history. If the outcome now seems to have been inevitable, that may be largely a confusion of the familiar with the necessary.

While Waite lived, Taney's tradition prevailed, but only against an engulfing cataract of Field's dissents. Within eight years after Appomattox, all but one of the pre-war justices had been replaced by Republicans. But

> their Republicanism was that of the Civil War period—a comparatively Jeffersonian Republicanism, idealistic and humane, with a faith in democracy that involved human dignity and independence [as well as] substantially of popular participation in the determination and control of public policy. . . . Some of the new justices had been lawyers for great financial interests. But practice had not yet become specialized. They had been lawyers for ordinary men as well. They shared the ordinary man's anxiety as to the effect upon him of industrial expansion and the concentration of wealth. . . . They wanted the great new United States to be rather an enlargement than a subversion of the United States in which they had grown up. That United States was in danger. How could it be saved without the help of legislation? Condi-

[9] For a more complete treatment see Wallace Mendelson, "Judicial Review and Party Politics," 12 Vanderbilt Law Review 447 (1959).

tions being new, legislation must be experimental. Legislative power must therefore be comparatively free.[10]

The Granger Movement illustrates the problem at the state level. A severe agricultural depression beginning in the early seventies followed the prosperity incidental to war and frenzied railroad expansion. Farmers discovered that freight charges were often discriminatory, if not extortionate. Rates in short were fixed by monopolists, not by competition. For relief the agrarians turned to state government and got the famous Granger legislation. This "hayseed socialism" raised for the first time in modern terms the classic problem of community "interference" with private enterprise deemed harmful to the public. More specifically, the *Granger Cases* raised for judicial determination the question of whether a state could regulate the rates charged by privately owned railroads and grain elevators. Ironically the Fourteenth Amendment—designed presumably to protect the Negro's freedom—served in the attempt to funnel this economic problem into the judicial arena. Chief Justice Waite and most of his associates found such matters more appropriate for political settlement: [11]

> When . . . one devotes his property to a use in which the public has an interest, he, in effect, grants to the public an interest in that use, and must submit to be controlled by the public for the common good, to the extent of the interest he has thus created. He may withdraw his grant by discontinuing the use; but, so long as he maintains the use, he must submit to the control. . . . We know that this [public power to regulate] . . . may be abused; but that is no argument against its existence. *For protection against abuses by legislatures the people must resort to the polls, not to the courts.* (Emphasis added).

This judicial reluctance to intrude upon legislative policy was pure Jeffersonianism handed down through Chief Justice Taney.

Mr. Justice Field, dissenting, voiced the old tradition that sprang from Hamilton, Marshall and Webster:

> The principle upon which the opinion of the majority proceeds is, in my judgment, subversive of the rights of private property. . . . The declaration of the [state] Constitution of 1870, that private buildings used for public purposes shall be deemed public institutions, does not

[10] Walter Nelles, Book Review, 40 Yale Law Journal 998, 999 (1931).
[11] *Munn* v. *Illinois,* 94 U.S. 113, 126–7 (1877).

make them so. . . . There is no magic in the language, though used by a constitutional convention, which can change a private business into a public one. . . . If this [the majority position] be sound law, if there be no protection, either in the principles upon which our republican government is founded, or in the prohibitions of the Constitution against such invasion of private rights, all property and all business in the State are held at the mercy of the majority of its legislature. . . . It is only where some right or privilege is conferred by the government . . . upon the owner, which he can use in connection with his property, or by means of which the use of his property is rendered more valuable to him, or he thereby enjoys an advantage over others, that the compensation to be received by him becomes a legitimate matter of regulation.

Of what avail is the constitutional provision that no state shall deprive any person of his property except by due process of law, if the state can, by fixing the compensation which he may receive for its use, take from him all that is valuable in the property?

A lower court judge had bitterly repudiated the claim that rate regulation was "an act of communism." In arguing before the Supreme Court, one of the railroad lawyers observed, "It is quite true that the theory of the statute is distinct from the doctrine of the communists. The latter divide property ratably between the plundered and the plunderers, while the former takes all for the Grangers."

To prevent such "communism," Field rested primarily upon the Fourteenth Amendment, and in later years particularly upon its Due Process Clause. Time after time, on circuit and dissenting in the Supreme Court, he repudiated the *Granger Cases,* until he finally won the day. If need be, he fell back upon the sanctity of corporate charters under the Contract Clause to prevent effective rate regulation.[12]

When dairy farmers, copying the antics of businessmen, succeeded in getting the economic equivalent of a tariff against (domestic) oleomargarine, their efforts were sustained by the Court. But Field in lone dissent found that the measure's validity "rested simply upon the fact that it has pleased the [state] legislature . . . to declare that the article shall not be manufactured or sold or kept for sale. . . ." That was not enough! The legislature should have been happy that science had discovered a new food. Field "had always supposed that the gift of life was accompanied with the

[12] *Spring Valley Water Works* v. *Shottler,* 110 U.S. 347, 376 (1884).

right to seek and produce food, by which life can be preserved and enjoyed. . . ." The liberty of the Due Process Clause means "something more than freedom from physical restraint or imprisonment," it includes the right to "pursue one's happiness." [13]

But one must not suppose that Field denied the existence of the so-called state police power. His concern rather was to bring it within specified, read judge-approved, boundaries. In *Munn* v. *Illinois*, for example, he said: [14]

> What is termed the police power of a state, which, from the language often used respecting it, one would suppose to be an undefined irresponsible element in government, can only interfere with the conduct of individuals in their intercourse with each other, and in the use of their property, so far as may be required to secure these objects [namely,] the peace, good order, morals and health of society. . . .

Thus, while it was irresponsible legislative whim to regulate oleomargarine and the rates charged by railroads, it was permissible to control alcoholic beverages [15] and penalize railroads for failing to erect cattle guards and fences along their rights of way. [16] For Field the distinction was so obvious [17] that in the latter case he repeated a caustic observation made earlier by Mr. Justice Miller—"there exists some strange misconception of the scope of this provision [the Due Process Clause] as found in the XIVth Amendment." It seems to be considered:

> as a means of bringing to the test of the decision of this Court the abstract opinions of every unsuccessful litigant in a state court, of the justice of the decision against him, and of the merits of the legislation on which such a decision may be founded.

[13] *Powell* v. *Pennsylvania,* 127 U.S. 678 (1888).

[14] 94 U.S. 113, 145 ff. (1877). As Mr. Justice Peckham put it, "When and how far such power may be legitimately exercised . . . must be left for determination to each case as it arises." *Allgeyer* v. *Louisiana,* 165 U.S. 578, 590 (1897).

[15] *Crowley* v. *Christensen,* 137 U.S. 86 (1890).

[16] *Missouri Pacific Ry.* v. *Humes,* 115 U.S. 512 (1885).

[17] "His working definition of the police power was a specification of permissible legislative objects: public health, peace, morals, education, good order, increase of industries, development of resources, and addition to wealth and prosperity. . . . In all his essays toward comprehensive definition of the police power the phrase 'general welfare' is conspicuous by its absence. Man by the social contract had granted to government no such roving commission." Walter Nelles *loc. cit.,* at 1003.

Doubtless there was such a "strange misconception" in the minds of many lawyers. It it impossible to think of anyone more responsible for feeding it than Mr. Justice Field. In a few years that "strange misconception" would be the law of the land.

The first national legislation to reach the Supreme Court in the post-bellum conflict between the farmer and the businessman involved the Greenbacks which Congress had authorized to help finance the Union Army. The agrarian, or "Ohio Idea," was that government bonds, having been purchased largely with that depreciated currency, should be repaid in the same medium. After all, it was the farmer (and labor) upon whom, under the prevailing regressive revenue system, the burden of repaying the bonds would ultimately fall. To business interests, the "Ohio Idea" was a "betrayal of national honor." But repayment of national bonds was only a small part of the problem. The real difficulty after 1865 was the steady thirty-year decline of farm commodity prices. That deflationary trend was the foundation of the persistent agrarian demand for "soft money."

Even Henry Carey, the famous contemporary economist who had endeared himself with businessmen by revamping classical economics to fit their demands for tariff "protection," supported the farm view: [18]

> A war upon what is called "paper money" is . . . a war upon the poor in favor of the rich; and that the war being made upon it has precisely that effect is proved by the fact, that the western farmer is now being so impoverished by reason of such a reduction in the price of corn and oats that the former is being used as fuel, while the latter sold at 8 cents a bushel [but] houses and lots in the neighborhood of Wall Street [are] commanding . . . prices such as had never before been heard of.

In "soft money" business interests saw nothing but heresy and more "hayseed socialism"—a complete violation of "sound business principles."

After a false start,[19] the agrarian position on the Greenback controversy had been upheld by the Supreme Court some three years before Waite took his seat upon the bench.[20] It was not un-

[18] Quoted in Vernon L. Parrington, *Main Currents in American Thought* (New York, Harcourt, Brace, 1927), Vol. 3, p. 110.

[19] *Hepburn* v. *Griswold,* 8 Wallace 603 (1870).

[20] *Legal Tender Cases,* 12 Wallace 457 (1871).

constitutional, at least as a war measure, for Congress to give paper money the quality of legal tender. Field and three associates had dissented vigorously. Thirteen years later the same issue was again before the Court, but this time there was no war emergency upon which to ground the action of Congress. For a majority, including Waite, the Necessary and Proper Clause (Article I, Sec. 8), as well as national sovereignty, was a sufficient foundation.[21] Here was constitutional sanction for the "embattled farmers," Greenback Party. Only Field dissented. Though he could find no provision in the Constitution which guarantees the sanctity of "contracts" vis-à-vis the national government, "justice" and the "universal law of currency" outlawed what Congress had done: [22]

> . . . for whenever it is declared that this government, ordained to establish justice, has the power to alter the condition of contracts between private parties, and authorize their payment or discharge in something different from that which the parties stipulated, thus disturbing the relations of commerce and the business of the community generally, the doctrine will not and ought not to be readily accepted. There will be many who will adhere to the teachings and abide by the faith of their fathers. So the question has come again, and will continue to come until it is settled so as to uphold and not impair the contracts of parties, to promote and not defeat justice. [After a discussion of the "universal law of currency," he proceeded.] From the decision of the Court I see only evil likely to follow.

Field's concern for the sanctity of contracts must have sounded a bit hollow to a wheat farmer, for example, who had encumbered himself with a mortgage when his produce was worth 76 cents a bushel (1869) and had to repay when it had steadily fallen to 49 cents (1894). His contract obligation had increased almost 65 per cent! No wonder some Easterners thought mortgages were the most important crop produced in the Middle West.

The same problems which gave rise to the Granger legislation also moved Congress to act. As of 1870, public land grants and gifts of money accounted for about 60 per cent of the cost of constructing our "private" railroads. A large part of the balance of that cost was met by the issuance of railroad bonds. The well known enormity of the corruption in railroad affairs led Congress to re-

[21] *Julliard* v. *Greenman,* 110 U.S. 421 (1884).
[22] *Id.* 451 ff.

quire that 25 per cent of the earnings of two congressionally chartered railways be set aside as a sinking fund for the retirement of their bonded indebtedness to the United States. There had been no such requirement in the original corporate charters, but finding that Congress had reserved the power to alter, amend or revoke them, Waite for a majority upheld the sinking fund legislation: [23]

Every possible presumption is in favor of the validity of a statute, and this continues until the contrary is shown beyond a rational doubt. One branch of government cannot encroach on the domain of another without danger. The safety of our institutions depends in no small degree on a strict observance of this salutary rule. . . . This corporation is a creature of the United States. It is a private corporation created for public purposes, and its property is to a large extent devoted to public uses. It is, therefore, subject to legislative control so far as its business affects the public interests. . . . It is unnecessary to decide what power Congress would have had over the charter if the right of amendment had not been reserved; for, as we think, that reservation has been made.

The United States cannot any more than a State interfere with private rights, except for legitimate governmental purposes. They are not included within the constitutional prohibition which prevents States from impairing the obligation of contracts, but equally with the States they are prohibited from depriving persons or corporations of property without due process of law. . . . The question still remains whether the particular provision of this statute . . . comes within this rule. [I]t is sufficient now to say that . . . the legislation complained of may be sustained on the ground that it is a reasonable regulation of the administration of the affairs of the corporation and promotive of the interests of the public and the corporators.

Field, dissenting with Justices Strong and Bradley, maintained: [24]

The decision will . . . tend to create insecurity in the title to corporate property in the country. It, in effect, determines that the general government, in its dealing with the Pacific Railroad Companies, is under no obligation to fulfill its contracts, and that whether it shall do so is a question of policy not of duty. . . . [The United States, having entered into a contract to loan the railroads money upon certain terms all of

[23] *Sinking Fund Cases,* 99 U.S. 700, 718 ff. (1879).
[24] *Id.* 750 ff.

which the debtor has met, cannot by the reserved power to alter, amend or repeal the debtor's corporate charter alter the terms of the indebtedness.] The object of a reservation of this kind in the acts of incorporation is to insure to the government control over corporate franchises, rights and privileges, which in its sovereign or legislative capacity, it may call into existence, not to interfere with contracts which the corporation created by it may make. . . . "The moment," said the elder Adams, "the idea is admitted into society that property is not as sacred as the laws of God, and that there is not a force of law and public justice to protect it, anarchy and tyranny commence."

While Chief Justice Waite lived, the tolerant view of legislation—state and natural—prevailed. Indeed, excepting Reconstruction measures,[25] the Court struck down little or nothing of substance that may be called social legislation. But the tide was clearly running the other way. Just prior to Waite's death in 1888, a majority of his associates were men whose constitutional thinking had been molded prior to the Civil War. Four of them had been born while Jefferson was still President, all of them before 1817. All were adults before Jackson left the White House. But in the decade following Waite's death in 1888, six new justices took their places upon the bench. Five of them constituted the majority "which decided the *Lochner* case in 1905. They were the products—the winnowed grain—of the Bar's self-indoctrination in the tenets of laissez-faireism" [26]—the products, that is, of the Gilded Age with its Great Barbecue for the Robber Barons and for the rest—"let the public be damned," as Mr. Vanderbilt is said to have put it.

Field's associate, Mr. Justice Miller—one of the great judges of the day—wrote to an intimate member of his family: [27]

It is vain to contend with judges who have been at the bar the advocates for forty years of railroad companies, and all the forms of associated capital, when they are called upon to decide cases where such interests are in contest. All their training, all their feelings are from the start in favor of those who need no such influence.

[25] See footnotes 39–41, below, and related text.

[26] Edward S. Corwin, *Liberty Against Government* (Baton Rouge, Louisiana State U.P., 1948), p. 146. See also Benjamin Twiss, *Lawyers and the Constitution* (Princeton, Princeton U.P., 1942).

[27] Reproduced in Charles Fairman, *Mr. Justice Miller and the Supreme Court* (Cambridge, Harvard U.P., 1939), p. 374.

And in the next paragraph we see why it is that the monumental perseverance of Field finally prevailed:

> I [Miller] am losing interest in these matters. I will do my duty but will *fight* no more. I am perhaps beginning to experience that loss of interest in many things which is the natural result of years and which wise men have felt the necessity of guarding against as age approaches.

Of course, "let-the-public-be-damned" was not imported into the Constitution overnight when Waite died. Field and three of his associates had struck a vigorous blow for it in *Munn* v. *Illinois*, to say nothing of *Hepburn* v. *Griswold*. Field stuck to his guns for the next generation, and while he was present no lawyer could be laughed out of court for urging it. Indeed, so great was the pressure from the bar and from within the Court that even Waite had to make at least linguistic concessions.[28] Building upon them, the Court gradually established doctrines which destroyed all that Waite had stood for. Within two years after his death, the crucial turning point came in the *Minnesota Commission* case of 1890.[29] The *Granger Cases* were not overruled in so many words, but it was established that the reasonableness of railroad rates was now a judicial question—no longer were disgruntled railroad lawyers referred to the polls for the "correction" of legislation which they found distasteful.

Field, now a sick old man, continued on the bench for another seven years, but seldom did he write an opinion after 1890. His fight was won; let younger men consolidate the position. The *Minnesota Commission* case led in due time to *Smyth* v. *Ames*.[30] Before Field died, his *Slaughter House*[31] and *Granger* dissents found expression in *Allgeyer* v. *Louisiana*[32] which in good time led to *Lochner* v. *New York*.[33] On the national level, all that Field had stood for in the *Legal Tender* and *Sinking Fund* cases was reflected in the decisions (Field concurring) which mutilated the Income

[28] The story is well told in Benjamin F. Wright, *The Growth of American Constitutional Law* (Boston, Houghton Mifflin, 1942), pp. 98 *et seq.*

[29] *Chicago, Milwaukee & St. Paul Ry.* v. *Minnesota*, 134 U.S. 418 (1890).

[30] 169 U.S. 466 (1898).

[31] *The Slaughter House Cases*, 16 Wallace 36 (1873).

[32] 165 U.S. 578 (1897).

[33] 198 U.S. 45 (1905).

Tax,[34] the Sherman Anti-Trust Act [35] and the Interstate Commerce Act.[36] Almost two generations of agrarian efforts to check the worst abuses of the "captains of industry" were destroyed by judicial action in the course of a few months. This was the foundation of the last great Jeffersonian revolt—Bryan's crusade of 1896.

So fearful was the "march of communism" in the Income Tax controversy that Field forsook his virtual retirement within the Court and wrote a forty-page concurring opinion—his swan song: [37]

> Here I close my opinion. I could not say less in view of questions of such gravity that go down to the very foundation of government. If the provisions of the Constitution can be set aside by an act of Congress, where is the course of usurpation to end? The present assault upon capital is but the beginning. It will be but the stepping-stone to others, larger and more sweeping, till our political contests will become a war of the poor against the rich; a war constantly growing in intensity and bitterness.

That half of his associates saw neither communism nor constitutional invalidity in the income tax—indeed that an earlier Court had sustained it [38]—deterred Field's assurance not a whit.

The agony of adjustment to economic revolution was only one legacy of the Civil War. Another concerned the scope of human freedom in the context of war and Reconstruction. Waite's (like Taney's) respect for the political processes as the proper solvent for economic problems was an expression of respect for democracy. The heart of democracy in turn is reverence for the individual. And so it is not surprising that the early post-bellum Court struck vigorous blows for personal liberty. *Ex parte Milligan* [39] upheld the civilian's right to trial by jury even for an essentially military offense. *Cummings* v. *Missouri* [40] sustained the right of clergymen

[34] *Pollock* v. *Farmers' Loan & Trust Co.*, 158 U.S. 601 (1895).

[35] *United States* v. *E. C. Knight Co.*, 165 U.S. 1 (1895).

[36] *ICC* v. *Alabama Midland Ry.*, 168 U.S. 144 (1897); *ICC* v. *Cincinnati, New Orleans and T.P. Ry.*, 167 U.S. 479 (1897); *Cincinnati, New Orleans and T.P. Ry.* v. *ICC*, 167 U.S. 479 (1897); *Cincinnati, New Orleans and T.P. Ry* v. *ICC*, 162 U.S. 184 (1896); *Texas and Pacific Ry* v. *ICC*, 162 U.S. 197 (1896).

[37] *Pollock* v. *Farmers Loan & Trust Co.*, 157 U.S. 429, 607 (1895).

[38] *Springer* v. *United States*, 102 U.S. 586 (1881).

[39] 4 Wallace 2 (1866).

[40] 4 Wallace 277 (1867).

and others to practice their professions without first swearing that they had always been loyal to the United States. *Ex parte Garland* [41] struck down an act of Congress imposing a similar "test oath" requirement upon attorneys seeking to practice in the federal courts. In *Yick Wo* v. *Hopkins* [42] the Court looked through the fair form of a California law to find effective racial discrimination against the Chinese. The measure was held invalid as a denial of the equal protection of the laws required by the Fourteenth Amendment. It is interesting that in these cases Field agreed with the Court. Indeed, he wrote the majority opinions in the "test oath" cases, and his courageous decisions [43] on circuit anticipated *Yick Wo*. Plainly, the Justice's "laissez-faire" was not confined to merely economic interests. It restrained governmental intrusion upon the individual in some other areas as well.

Now the fateful problem of the emancipated Negro. The Thirteenth Amendment abolished slavery. But, if the old system died as a legal institution, many of its social, economic and political incidents survived. To limit at least some of these was the main purpose of the Fourteenth and Fifteenth Amendments. Chief Justice Waite's Court recognized and staunchly enforced this purpose. As it said in *Strauder* v. *West Virginia*: [44]

> The true spirit and meaning of the amendments, as we said in the Slaughter House Cases . . . cannot be understood without keeping in view the history of the times when they were adopted, and the general objects they plainly sought to accomplish. At the time when they were incorporated in the Constitution, it required little knowledge of human nature to anticipate that those who had long been regarded as an inferior and subject race would, when suddenly raised to the rank of citizenship, be looked upon with jealousy and positive dislike, and that State laws might be enacted or enforced to perpetuate the distinctions that had before existed. Discriminations against them had been habitual. It is well known that in some States laws making such discriminations then existed, and others might well be expected. The colored race, as a race, was abject and ignorant, and in that condition was unfitted to command the respect of those who had superior intelligence. Their

[41] 4 Wallace 333 (1867).

[42] 118 U.S. 356 (1886).

[43] *Ho Ah Kow* v. *Nunan*, 5 Sawyer 552 (Cal. 1879); *In re Ah Fong*, 3 Sawyer 144 (Cal. 1874).

[44] 100 U.S. 303 (1880).

training had left them mere children, and as such they needed the protection which a wise government extends to those who are unable to protect themselves. They especially needed protection against unfriendly action in the States where they were resident. It was in view of these considerations that the Fourteenth Amendment was framed and adopted. It was designed to assure to the colored race the enjoyment of all civil rights that under the law are enjoyed by white persons, and to give to that race the protection of the general government, in that enjoyment, whenever it should be denied by the States. ***The very fact that colored people are singled out and expressly denied by a statute all right to participate in the administration of the law, as jurors, because of their color, though they are citizens, and may be in other respects fully qualified, is practically a brand upon them, affixed by the law, an assertion of their inferiorty, and a stimulant to that race prejudice which is an impediment to securing to individuals of the race that equal justice which the law aims to secure to all others.

It followed that, since the state law barring Negroes from jury service was invalid, conviction of a Negro thereunder was also invalid.

The *Strauder* principles grew in *Ex parte Virginia* [45] to cover discrimination embedded not in legislation, but in the action of a state trial judge. Indeed the Supreme Court found that the offending judge had "acted outside his authority and in direct violation of the spirit of the State statute." Even so, this was held to be forbidden *state* action within the meaning of the Fourteenth Amendment. Accordingly the judge was punishable under the federal Civil Rights Act.[46]

Mr. Justice Field dissented in both cases! And here too, as in *Munn* v. *Illinois,* the spirit of his views became the law of the land before he left the bench. Of course, the "separate-but-equal" rule of *Plessy* v. *Ferguson* [47] in 1896 did not overrule *Strauder* and *Ex parte Virginia.* Neither did the *Minnesota Commission* case, nor *Smyth* v. *Ames,* explicitly disavow *Munn* v. *Illinois.* Yet there can be no doubt that in both areas the later cases limit, if they do not fully undermine, the Court's earlier position. Justices Harlan and Field were the only judges who participated in *Strauder* and *Ex*

45 100 U.S. 339 (1880).

46 A congressional measure enacted pursuant to Sec. 5 of the Fourteenth Amendment.

47 163 U.S. 537 (1896).

parte Virginia as well as *Plessy*. Field, who had dissented in the earlier cases in 1880, was with the majority in 1896. Harlan, who had been with the majority in the earlier cases, dissented in 1896. These two remained constant; the Court had changed.

Evidently Mr. Justice Field was more sensitive than most of his colleagues on Waite's Court to the temper of the times. America's attention had turned from slavery to industrial expansion, from the demands of the soul to the demands of the flesh, from the Declaration of Independence to The Gospel of Wealth. Henry Adams called it "the degradation of the democratic dogma" [48] and observed that "The progress of evolution from President Washington to President Grant was alone evidence enough to upset Darwin." [49]

After some resistance the Supreme Court responded to the sea-change. Just as it surrendered to "laissez-faire," so it *simultaneously* surrendered to racial segregation. In an age preoccupied with making money, "reconstruction" could only hinder the real business at hand. An ossified political party system frustrated effective popular government.[50] This was an open invitation to the old Hamiltonian ideal of control by the influential few—fortified, if need be, by Judicial Supremacy.

In his brilliant volume on *Reunion and Reaction*, C. V. Woodward has shown that the "Bargain of 1877" involved far more than withdrawal of Union troops from the South, in exchange for Hayes in the White House. In its full reach, it was an extra-party alliance between Northern and Southern Bourbons—an alliance that has persisted off and on ever since. In the face of the flagrantly corrupt Grant Administration, the Southern upper-crust insured continued Republican control of national affairs, for a share of the spoils. These included a cabinet post (the Postmaster Generalship, no less, with attendant patronage), "internal improvements," subsidy for a southern transcontinental railroad (the Texas and Pacific),—as well as "home rule" (freedom to "keep the Negro in his place"). When Northern Republicanism had to choose between protection

[48] Henry Adams, *The Degradation of the Democratic Dogma* (New York, Smith Peter, 1959).

[49] *The Education of Henry Adams* (Boston, Houghton Mifflin, 1918), p. 266.

[50] What Professor Holcombe calls *The New Party Politics* (as distinct from the classical sectional politics) had not yet arisen. See Chap. VI, below, footnotes 2 and 3, and related text.

for the Negro and Hamiltonianism (tariff, "hard" money, national bank, regressive taxes, and lush business subsidies) it chose the latter.

After a customary judicial lag, the spirit of 1877 found expression in a rebirth of Judicial Supremacy. Just as the "bargain" freed the South from political Reconstruction, *Plessy* v. *Ferguson* (1896) preserved it from constitutional (judicial) reconstruction. Both saved Northern business from the distraction of an issue that had out-lived its day—and perhaps served its purpose. Just as the "bargain" provided political pelf for Bourbons, so the *Income Tax, Anti-Trust, Labor Injunction* [51] and *Railroad Rate* cases (1895–1898) provided judicial spoils. In short, the Gilded Age and the Great Barbecue finally infected the judiciary. No institution can long resist the morality of its age.

In this light, Mr. Justice Field and the Court which eventually followed him most of the way are comprehensible. Not logic, but the *Zeitgeist* explains how a judge could find protection in the Fourteenth Amendment for Chinese aliens, but not for Negro citizens.[52] It was only a surface paradox for Field to insist that the Civil War Amendments guaranteed a butcher's "right" to ply his trade, but not a Negro's right to trial by jury free from racial discrimination.[53] Separate-but-equal, of course, did not go quite so far. But it was a master stroke. The "equal" element provided something for the Northern conscience; the "separate" aspect was for the South. Who but the impotent victims would care if in practice separation destroyed even the pretense of equality? After all "more important" things were stirring and demanding all available energy.

By the end of Field's career, the legal foundations of "laissez-faire" capitalism were firmly entrenched in the Constitution. The old rival plantation economy had been destroyed. Middle Western efforts to check some of the worst abuses of Hamiltonianism were throttled after 1888 by Judicial Supremacy. Emasculation of the Interstate Commerce Commission left railroads free to continue their old practices without state [54] or national interference. Trusts

[51] *In re Debs,* 158 U.S. 564 (1895).

[52] Compare Field's positions in *Yick Wo* and *Ex parte Virginia.*

[53] Compare Field's positions in *The Slaughter House Cases* and *Ex parte Virginia.*

[54] *Wabash, St. Louis & Pacific Ry.* v. *Illinois,* 118 U.S. 557 (1886).

had substantial immunity from prosecution, and their ill-got profits were tax-exempt. Elimination of the income tax as an alternate source of federal revenue destroyed hope for tariff reform. Farmers and laboring-men—white and black—paid the bill. They were saddled as consumers with the cost of monopoly as well as the cost of government. Such was the practical socio-economic result of the judicial revolution which Field led.

Obviously Jeffersonianism had lost the day. The old agrarian ideal had become an anachronism in the Gilded Age. The farmer's role as opposition leader was gradually passing into the hands of labor, though it was obvious that a Court which could checkmate the political efforts of the one need not surrender before the more direct self-help of the other. Indeed, "government by injunction" received the sanction of the Supreme Court—Field concurring—in the same Term that undermined the anti-trust law and the income tax.[55]

By the time of his retirement in 1897, Field's angry dissents of the seventies and eighties were the law of the land, and the seeds were set for another judicial revolution, which came exactly forty years later. Meanwhile another great dissenter—Oliver Wendell Holmes—came to the Supreme Court in 1902, three years after Field's death. He would spend a lifetime attempting to give his colleagues an "education in the obvious," namely, that to read their economic prejudices into the Constitution was not the proper function of judges.

[55] *In re Debs*, 158 U.S. 564 (1895).

V

MR. JUSTICE HOLMES

Humility, Skepticism, and Democracy

Character is fate, and so is circumstance. A great man is one whose personal qualities satisfy the pressing needs of a particular engagement in the continuing campaign of history. Early in the twentieth century, Oliver Wendell Holmes brought to the Supreme Court of the nation two striking qualities: skepticism, and intellectual humility—perfect solvents for the economic dogmatism which under the mask of Natural or Higher Law had permeated both bench and bar. In the preceding quarter of a century the judiciary had got into the habit of treating Adam Smith

as though his generalizations had been imparted to him on Sinai, and not as a thinker who addressed himself to the elimination of restrictions which had become fetters upon initiative and enterprise in his day. Basic human rights expressed by the constitutional conception of liberty were equated with theories of laissez-faire. . . . The result was that economic views of confined validity were treated by lawyers and judges as though the Framers had enshrined them in the Constitution. This misapplication of the notions of the classic economists and resulting disregard of the perduring reach of the Constitution [1]

was strangling the growth of the nation and frustrating the processes of democracy.

In origin, laissez-faire was a reaction to mercantilism. It contemplated a termination of governmental handouts for business.

[1] *See* Mr. Justice Frankfurter in *A. F. of L.* v. *American Sash & Door Co.*, 335 U.S. 538, 542 (1949).

The economy was to stand on its own feet independent of tariffs, monopolistic grants, special trading privileges, and other public bounties. It was in this sense that Jefferson and Jackson—radicals in their day—had sponsored the philosophy of laissez-faire. But to fight one's battles under the enemy's banner is an old strategy. By the end of the nineteenth century, businessmen had taken over laissez-faire for their own, twisting it into a defense against democratic efforts to regulate business for the protection of the public. For in the interim since Jackson's day, de Tocqueville's prophesy had proven true; the masses refused "to remain miserable and sovereign." And so it happened, as Bryce observed in 1888, that "one-half of the capitalists are occupied in preaching laissez-faire as regards railroad control, the other in resisting it—in tariff matters. . . . Yet they manage to hold well together." Businessmen found their great spokesman in an English philosopher-biologist, Herbert Spencer, who incidentally was "rejected by professional philosophers as superficial and by scientists as ignorant." In his hands, Darwin's struggle for existence and survival of the fittest became a natural law of social organization. As such, it provided cosmic justification for the Robber Barons' greedy exploitation of the nation's human and geographic resources. "Their cupidity, it defended as part of the universal struggle for existence; their wealth, it hallowed as the sign of the fittest." Governmental interference for the protection of the public was a violation of nature and as such doomed to bring more hardship than good, for "the poverty of the incapable, the distresses that come upon the improvident, the starvation of the idle, and the shouldering aside of the weak by the strong, which leaves so many in shadows and misery are the decrees of a large, far-seeing benevolence. . . ." [2] As a present day Congressman put it, "Every one for himself, said the elephant, as he danced among the chickens."

When Mr. Justice Holmes took his seat upon the Supreme Court bench in 1902, this pseudo-laissez-faire had been absorbed into the law of the land, particularly into the Due Process Clause of the Fourteenth Amendment. In its spirit, the judiciary had frustrated numerous popular efforts to mitigate the more obvious

[2] This and the foregoing non-footnoted quotations appear in Alpheus T. Mason, *Free Government in the Making* (New York, Oxford U.P., 1949), Ch. 16.

abuses of the American industrial revolution. Specifically during the last five years of the nineteenth century, the Supreme Court had destroyed or emasculated legislative attempts to control monopoly,[3] prevent unfair railroad rates,[4] tax income[5] or regulate utilities[6] and insurance companies.[7] But while "laissez-faire" on the bench meant exemption of business from the processes of democratic government, it subjected workingmen to extra-democratic processes, namely, government by injunction.[8] Thus the standard was double, working uniformly for the benefit of those who by popular standards already had too many advantages. President Hadley revealed the temper of the times when he claimed that "the fundamental division of powers in the Constitution of the United States is between voters on the one hand and property owners on the other. The forces of democracy on the one side, divided between the executive and the legislature, are set over against the forces of property on the other side with the judiciary as arbiter between them. . . ."[9]—which was, of course, the way Hamiltonians looked at it. For to make "laissez-faire" the "arbiter" between democracy and property meant the latter would win all engagements. As Mr. Justice Holmes put it,[10]

> I suspect that this fear [of "socialism" on the part of the "comfortable classes"] has influenced judicial action both here and in England. . . . I think that something similar has led people who no longer hope to control the legislatures to look to the courts as expounders of the Constitutions, and that in some courts new principles have been discovered outside of the bodies of those instruments, which may be generalized into acceptance of the economic doctrines which prevailed about fifty years ago, and a wholesale prohibition of what a tribunal of lawyers does not think about right.

The judicial genius of Holmes did not lie in a questioning of

[3] *United States* v. *E. C. Knight Co.*, 156 U.S. 1 (1895).

[4] Maximum Rate Case, 167 U.S. 479 (1897); Social Circle Case, 162 U.S. 184 (1896); *Texas & Pacific Ry.* v. *I.C.C.*, 162 U.S. 197 (1896).

[5] *Pollock* v. *Farmers' Loan & Trust Co.*, 158 U.S. 601 (1895).

[6] *Smyth* v. *Ames*, 169 U.S. 466 (1898).

[7] *Allgeyer* v. *Louisiana*, 165 U.S. 578 (1897).

[8] *In re Debs*, 158 U.S. 564 (1895).

[9] Mason, *op. cit.*, Ch. 16.

[10] Holmes, *The Path of the Law* in Collected Legal Papers (New York, Harcourt, Brace, 1920), p. 184.

the new "laissez-faire".[11] For while he was apt to express himself more subtly than spokesmen for the Robber Barons, it is clear that he was in fundamental agreement with them on the major tenets of Spencerian doctrine. The Justice was a true product of the age of Darwin. For him "the struggle for life is the order of the world . . . man's destiny in battle." [12] He put his hopes in racial improvement, not in alterations of human institutions. Time after time he repeated Spencer's warning that in society, as in mechanics, there is no way to get something for nothing. Human efforts to ameliorate the "struggle for existence" merely beget new woes (or rather shift old ones) and society must inevitably foot the bill. Hence the deep Holmesian skepticism towards reform and especially reformers—"cock-sure of a thousand reforms," "the greatest bores in the world:"

> The social reformers of today seem to me so far to forget that we no more can get something for nothing by legislation than we can by mechanics as to be satisfied if the bill to be paid for their improvements is not presented in a lump sum. Interstitial detriments that may far outweigh the benefit promised are not bothered about. Probably I am too skeptical as to our ability to do more than shift disagreeable burdens from the shoulders of the stronger to those of the weaker. . . . I believe that the wholesale social regeneration which so many now seem to expect, if it can be helped by conscious, coordinated human effort, cannot be affected appreciably by tinkering with the institution of property, but only by taking in hand life and trying to build a race. . . . The notion that with socialized property we should have women free and a piano for everybody seems to be an empty humbug.[13]

> . . . most of the enlightened reformers . . . seem to me not to have considered with accuracy the means at our disposal and to become rhetorical where I want figures. The notion that we can secure an economic paradise by changes in property alone seem to me twaddle. I can understand better legislation that aims rather to improve the quality . . . of the population. If before the English factory acts the race was

[11] Holmes-Pollock Letters, Howe, M.D., ed. (Cambridge, Harvard U.P., 1941), p. 309. Acceptance of laissez-faire is implicit in many of his opinions and other writings.

[12] Speeches (Boston, Little Brown, 1934), p. 58.

[13] Oliver W. Holmes, *Ideals and Doubts* in Collected Legal Papers (New York, Harcourt, Brace, 1920), pp. 305–306.

running down physically I can understand taking the economic risk of passing those acts—although they had to be paid for, and I do not doubt in some way or other England was worse off for them, however favorable the balance of account. I can understand a man's saying in any case, I want this or that and I am willing to pay the price, if he realizes what the price is. What I most fear is saying the same thing when those who say it do not know and have made no serious effort to find out what it will cost, as I think we in this country are rather inclined to do.[14]

But, fundamentally in accord with the doctrines of laissez-faire, Holmes had learned what Morris Cohen called "the great lesson of life," namely, humility. And so, man and judge, he refused to act as though he, or indeed anyone, held an exclusive compass of truth:

When I say a thing is true, I mean that I cannot help believing it. I am stating an experience as to which there is no choice. But as there are many things that I cannot help doing that the universe can, I do not venture to assume that my inabilities in the way of thought are inabilities of the universe. I therefore define truth as the system of my limitations, and leave absolute truth for those who are better equipped. . . . To have doubted one's own first principles is the mark of a civilized man.[15]

Certitude is not the test of certainty. We have been cock-sure of many things that were not so. . . . What we most love and revere generally is determined by early associations. . . . But while one's experience thus makes certain preferences dogmatic for one's self, recognition of how they came to be so leaves one able to see that others, poor souls, may be equally dogmatic about something else.[16]

It is this humility, this refusal to read his own experiences and beliefs into the Constitution, and his alertness in opposing judicial associates who, often unconsciously, did so, that constitutes the genius of Holmes. He did not confuse his personal tastes and distastes with constitutional necessity. And so when his associates read a pseudo-laissez-faire into the law of the land, and showed marked hostility to offensive speech, Holmes was apt to be in dissent. But he was outspokenly skeptical of the reforms involved

[14] Reproduced in Max Lerner, *The Mind and Faith of Mr. Justice Holmes* (Boston, Little Brown, 1943), pp. 400–401.

[15] Oliver W. Holmes, *Ideals and Doubts* in Collected Legal Papers (New York, Harcourt, Brace, 1920), pp. 304, 307.

[16] *Id.* at 311.

in most of the great opinions which he wrote in support of legislative freedom to adopt them; as in the famous free speech dissents he openly disdained the ideas whose utterance he defended. Thus on a bedrock of humility and skepticism Holmes laid the foundation for an abiding democratic philosophy.

Just as he would allow experiments in economics which he himself viewed with doubt and distrust, so he would protect speech that offended his taste and wisdom. At bottom both attitudes came from a central faith and a governing skepticism. Since the whole truth has not yet been, and is not likely to be, brought up from its bottomless well, the first duty of an educated man was to doubt his major premise even while he continued to act upon it. This was the skeptical conviction with which he distrusted dogma, whether economic or intellectual. But his was never the paralyzing skepticism which easily becomes comfortable or corroding cynicism. He had a positive faith—faith in the gradual power to pierce nature's mysteries through man's indomitable endeavors. This was the road by which he reached an attitude of widest tolerance toward views which were strange and uncongenial to him, lest by a premature stifling even of crude or groping ideas society might be deprived of eventual wisdom for attaining a gracious civilization.[17]

In a word, free speech, press and assembly are indispensable tools of democratic self-government for they safeguard society's thinking process. And so it is one thing for judges to protect free expression from legislative mutilation; to strike down the legislative fruits which free expression bears in the economic realm—wage and hour laws, for example—is something quite different. For neither democracy nor free expression have meaning, if judges are to substitute their views for those adopted by a community whose channels of discussion and thought are unobstructed.

From that premise spring the two famous rules—clear and present danger and reasonable man—which Holmes urged for guiding and limiting judges in the exercise of their power of judicial review: the power, that is, to impede the forces of democracy, to block the rights of self-government. For it seemed to the Justice that, "as the decisions now stand, . . . [there is] hardly any limit but the sky to the invalidating of those rights if they happen to strike a majority of this Court as for any reason undesirable." [18]

[17] Felix Frankfurter, *Mr. Justice Holmes and the Supreme Court* (Cambridge, Harvard U.P., 1938), pp. 61–62.
[18] *See Baldwin* v. *Missouri,* 281 U.S. 586, 595 (1930).

The more fundamental of Holmes' two famous rules was that designed to determine the bounds of what men may say or write in a democratic society. To be sure, the First Amendment speaks in absolute terms—"Congress shall make no law . . . abridging" free discussion. But life and society are dynamic processes which neither we, nor the Founding Fathers, could hope to imprison in a phrase of a dozen words. In constitutions particularly it is the essence behind the words that counts; often "the letter killeth." The function of the great judge is to "preserve his authority by cloaking himself in the majesty of an overshadowing past; but he must discover some composition with the dominant trends of his time—at all hazards he must maintain that tolerable continuity without which society dissolves, and man must begin again the weary path up from savagery." [19]

Looking behind the simple language of the First Amendment, Holmes found in its free expression provisions a plain purpose—to safeguard society's thinking process; no more and no less. Thus he who seeks to *debate* public issues is protected, however outrageous a judge or legislature may find his views. But he who would incite improper action, though he do so via speech, has no claim to immunity from punishment or prohibition. Falsely crying fire in a crowded theater is not calculated to start an intellectual discussion. It is no part of the process by which truth is brought up from its bottomless well; hence like other anti-social action, it is subject to public restraint. The extreme cases are always easy. It is in the penumbra that the line is difficult to trace. To distinguish between discussion words and "words that may have all the effect of force" Holmes, in the case of *Schenck* v. *United States,* devised the clear and present danger rule:

> . . . the character of every act depends upon the circumstances in which it was done. . . . The most stringent protection of free speech would not protect a man in falsely shouting fire in a theater, and causing a panic. It does not even protect a man from an injunction against uttering words that may have all the effect of force. . . . The question in every case is whether the words used are used in such circumstances and are of such a nature as to create a clear and present danger that they

[19] Learned Hand, *Mr. Justice Cardozo,* 48 Yale Law Journal 379 (1939).

will bring about the substantive evils that Congress has a right to prevent. It is a question of proximity and degree.[20]

That was the first laconic statement of principle. Thereafter, in a series of brilliant dissents and separate concurring opinions,[21] Justices Holmes and Brandeis spelled out some of its implications in language that is not apt to be forgotten.

It is noteworthy that after the *Schenck* case, while Holmes and Brandeis were on the bench, no other Justice supported the danger rule. In five more Espionage Act cases [22] decided in 1919–1920, the *Schenck* decision was cited by the Court as controlling, but the danger test was hardly mentioned and none of the evidence was analyzed in danger terms. In each instance convictions were sustained. Thus, for all but one of his associates, Holmes' formula apparently was an acceptable device for sending men to jail and nothing more. In the throes of World War I and its aftermath, when free speech was jeopardized by popular hysteria as never before in American history, a majority of the Justices were willing to uphold punishment for speech merely because of its supposed "bad tendency." [23]

Progress marches with the sword of criticism and must of necessity threaten anguish for the status quo. From time immemorial its "tendency" has been "bad." And so Holmes saw

misfortune if a judge reads his conscious or unconscious sympathy with one side or the other prematurely into the law, and forgets that what seem to him to be first principles are believed by half his fellow men to be wrong. I think that we have suffered from this misfortune . . . and that this is another very important truth to be extracted from the popular discontent. When twenty years ago a vague terror went over the earth and the word socialism began to be heard, I thought and

[20] 249 U.S. 47 (1919).

[21] *Whitney* v. *California*, 274 U.S. 357 (1927); *Gitlow* v. *New York*, 268 U.S. 652 (1925); *Gilbert* v. *Minnesota*, 254 U.S. 325 (1920); *Pierce* v. *United States*, 252 U.S. 239 (1920); *Schaefer* v. *United States*, 251 U.S. 468 (1920); *Abrams* v. *United States*, 250 U.S. 616 (1919).

[22] *Debs* v. *United States*, 249 U.S. 211 (1919); *Frowerk* v. *United States*, 249 U.S. 204 (1919); *Abrams* v. *United States*, 250 U.S. 616 (1919); *Schaefer* v. *United States*, 251 U.S. 468 (1920); *Pierce* v. *United States*, 252 U.S. 239 (1920). In *Gitlow* v. *New York*, 268 U.S. 652 (1925) the court mentioned the danger test only to distinguish it to permit upholding a conviction.

[23] This position is seen most clearly in *Gitlow* v. *New York*, 268 U.S. 652 (1925).

still think that fear was translated into doctrines that had no proper place in the Constitution or the common law. Judges are apt to be naive, simple-minded men, and they need something of Mephistopheles. We too need education in the obvious—to learn to transcend our own convictions and to leave room for much that we hold dear to be done away with short of revolution by the orderly change of law.[24]

But Mr. Justice Brandeis, more fervent, more loquacious and more disposed to stoop for detail than Holmes, gave the clear and present danger rule its ultimate formulation: [25]

> Those who won our independence believed that the final end of the State was to make men free to develop their faculties; and that in its government the deliberative forces should prevail over the arbitrary. . . . They believed that freedom to think as you will and speak as you think are means indispensable to the discovery and spread of political truth; that without free speech and assembly discussion would be futile; that with them, discussion affords ordinarily adequate protection against the dissemination of noxious doctrine. . . . they knew that it is hazardous to discourage thought, hope and imagination; that fear breeds repression; that repression breeds hate; that hate menaces stable government; that without free speech and assembly discussion would be futile; that the path to safety lies in the opportunity to discuss freely supposed grievances and proposed remedies; and that the fitting remedy for evil counsels is good ones. Believing in the power of reason as applied through public discussion, they eschewed silence coerced by law—the argument of force in its worst form.
>
> Fear of serious injury cannot alone justify suppression of free speech and assembly. Men feared witches and burnt women. It is the function of free speech to free men from the bondage of irrational fears. To justify suppression of free speech there must be reasonable ground to fear that serious evil will result if free speech is practiced. There must be reasonable ground to believe that the danger apprehended is imminent. There must be reasonable ground to believe that the evil to be prevented is a serious one. Every denunciation of existing law tends in some measure to increase the probability that there will be violation of it. Condonation of a breach enhances the probability. Propagation of the criminal state of mind by teaching syndicalism increases it. Advocacy of law-breaking heightens it still further. But even advocacy of violation, however reprehensible morally, is not a justification for denying free speech where the advocacy falls short of incitement and there

[24] Speeches (Boston, Little Brown, 1934), pp. 101–102.
[25] *Whitney* v. *California*, 274 U.S. 357 (1927).

is nothing to indicate that the advocacy would be immediately acted on. The wide difference between advocacy and incitement, between preparation and attempt, between assembling and conspiracy must be borne in mind. In order to support a finding of clear and present danger it must be shown either that immediate serious violence was to be expected or was advocated, or that the past conduct furnished reason to believe that such advocacy was then contemplated.

Those who won our independence by revolution were not cowards. They did not fear political change. They did not exalt order at the cost of liberty. To courageous, self-reliant men, with confidence in the power of free and fearless reasoning applied through the processes of popular government, no danger flowing from speech can be deemed clear and present, unless the incidence of the evil apprehended is so imminent that it may befall before there is opportunity for full discussion. If there be time to expose through discussion the falsehood and fallacies, to avert the evil by the processes of education, the remedy to be applied is more speech, not enforced silence. Only an emergency can justify repression. Such must be the rule if authority is to be reconciled with freedom. Such, in my opinion, is the command of the Constitution. It is therefore always open to Americans to challenge a law abridging free speech and assembly by showing that there was no emergency justifying it.

Moreover, even imminent danger cannot justify resort to prohibition of these functions essential to effective democracy, unless the evil apprehended is relatively serious. Prohibition of free speech is a measure so stringent that it would be inappropriate as the means for averting a relatively trivial harm to society.

The upshot of this position then was that advocacy is to be free up to that last possible point where it merges into action so immediately dangerous that there is no opportunity for the democratic corrective of counter discussion.

When men have realized that time has upset many fighting faiths, they may come to believe, even more than they believe the very foundations of their own conduct, that the ultimate good desired is better reached by free trade in ideas,—that the best test of truth is the power of the thought to get itself accepted in the competition of the market, and that truth is the only ground upon which their wishes safely can be carried out. [26]

But the insights, even the rhetoric, of the master often become dogma in the hands of his disciples. For Holmes, in contrast to some

[26] *Abrams* v. *United States*, 250 U.S. 616 (1919).

of his successors, the precept of clear and present danger was one of limited applicability. The Justice used it as a guide for judges in the application of espionage and criminal syndicalism statutes to particular factual situations—an adaptation of the common-law principles of incitement to crime. Unfettered discussion is "essential to democracy," but inducing illegal action is not. The danger rule was Holmes' litmus for fixing the point at which words cease to be "keys of persuasion" and become "triggers of [illegal] action." But he neither held nor implied that incitement to crime was the only basis for restraint of utterance. That was merely a particular application of a general principle, namely, that democracy need not tolerate abuse or perversion of its freedoms.

Certainly there are many abuses which cannot be measured in terms of incitement and danger. When a state's interests in educating its youngsters in English was subsumed by the Court to a Lutheran parochial school teacher's interest in teaching and expressing himself in German, Mr. Justice Holmes dissented on reasonable basis grounds.[27] He did not attempt to weigh the conflicting interests in danger test terms as some of his successors did in the comparable Flag Salute litigation.[28] That the danger test reveals no imminent danger (abuse) in such circumstances is no more significant than failure of a barometer to disclose an impending avalanche, Holmes' danger test is meaningless in contexts where there is no problem of inducement or incitement to crime.

Of course the Constitution does not protect "force-words," but neither does it forbid majorities to be "foolish." It merely requires that dissenters be free to make the most of such "foolishness" argumentatively. Forbidding "free speech" in German did not hobble society's thinking process. No ideas were repressed. No

[27] *Meyers* v. *Nebraska,* 262 U.S. 390 (1923).

[28] *West Virginia Bd. of Education* v. *Barnette,* 319 U.S. 624 (1943). The public interest involved is much the same in both cases, though the private interests differ somewhat. The Flag Salute was treated as a problem of religious freedom, while in the *Meyer* case the economic interest of the teacher was emphasized, though there are clear civil liberty overtones. The emphasis on economics is explained by the fact that as of 1923 the Court had not yet been willing to bring civil liberty within the protection of the Fourteenth Amendment. When it did so two years later, the *Meyer* case and *Pierce* v. *Society of Sisters,* 268 U.S. 510 (1925) based upon it, "cleared the ground" for that result. Zechariah Chafee, *Free Speech in the United States* (Cambridge, Harvard U.P., 1941), pp. 321–322.

one was denied liberty to participate in the political processes, nor to attempt to change public opinion. In short the purpose of the free expression clauses was not violated. Similarly on the Massachusetts Supreme Court Holmes upheld as reasonable state efforts to forbid certain political activities by policemen [29] and to restrict speech-making on Boston Commons.[30] Clearly the Justice distinguished between restriction on ideas and mere regulation of modes of expression. Only when the governmental thrust was against an idea as such did Holmes apply the danger test—his purpose being to give ideas full protection up to that final point where they merge into misconduct. But when the public animus was not censorious in purpose or substantial effect, when it was directed merely against impropriety in terms of time, place or manner of expression, Holmes' criterion was the less stringent reasonable-man test.[31]

"Congress [like the states] certainly cannot forbid all effort to change the mind of the country." [32] The democratic political processes require substantial opportunity for public discussion of all ideas. But those processes are not materially impeded when, for example, the public sets aside a park to furnish opportunity for repose free from political or religious polemics.[33] The most that a court may ask in such circumstances is whether there are reasonable opportunities for adequate public discussion elsewhere.

When after a long period of neglect the danger approach was resurrected by a quartet of libertarians in the 1940's, the distinction between restraints upon a speaker's mind and restraints upon his manners was lost. The resulting perversion of Holmes' danger test into a formula of general coverage is a source of much of the "Roosevelt Court's" civil-liberty trouble, threatening such anarchic results as "trial by newspaper" [34] and a proselytizer's "right" to

[29] *McAuliffe* v. *New Bedford,* 155 Mass. 216 (1891).

[30] *Commonwealth* v. *Davis,* 162 Mass. 510 (1895).

[31] Holmes' vote in *Pierce* v. *Society of Sisters,* 268 U.S. 510 (1925) seems to indicate simply that he saw in the Ku Klux Klan inspired legislation there involved more than a mere attempt to regulate modes of expression.

[32] *Abrams* v. *United States,* 250 U.S. 616, 628 (1919).

[33] *Commonwealth* v. *Davis,* 162 Mass. 510 (1895); *cf. Kovacs* v. *Cooper,* 336 U.S. 77 (1949); *Saia* v. *New York,* 334 U.S. 558 (1948).

[34] See the *Times-Mirror* case, Chapter VI, below.

invade the privacy of the home.[35] The danger test is simply not sensitive to an avalanche of non-violent abuse, nor was it designed to be. Censoring ideas is one thing; reasonable regulation of the time, place and manner of expression is something else.

Just as Holmes tried to narrow the permissible range of legislative censorship, he sought simultaneously to leave broad scope for legislative experiments in economic control. His double standard was grounded both in the meaning of democracy and the language of the Constitution. For the First Amendment speaks in plainer terms than do the Due Process Clauses.[36] Indeed any economic content which the court "found" in Due Process it put there. Only very late in the history of that ancient concept did it become the embodiment of the dogmas of pseudo-laissez-faire. Such improvisation by the judicial process of inclusion and exclusion, such bald, unlimited Constitution-making by judges in defiance of universal democratic trends was more than Holmes could abide: [37]

> The Fourteenth Amendment does not enact Mr. Herbert Spencer's Social Statics. . . . Some of these laws embody convictions or prejudices which judges are likely to share. Some may not. But a constitution is not intended to embody a particular economic theory, whether of paternalism and the organic relation of the citizen to the State or of laissez faire. It is made for people of fundamentally differing views, and the accident of our finding certain opinions natural and familiar or novel and even shocking ought not to conclude our judgment upon the question whether statutes embodying them conflict with the Constitution of the United States.

For many, perhaps most, of its ardent advocates "States' rights" does not mean freedom for a state to govern itself. They use the term merely as a club to defeat national legislation. For when states do attempt positively to use their reserved powers, "states' righters" are apt to be among the first to denounce the effort as an

[35] *Martin* v. *Struthers,* 319 U.S. 141 (1943). But see *Breard* v. *Alexandria,* 341 U.S. 622 (1951).

[36] As to Holmes' grounds for reading free speech into the Due Process Clause of the Fourteenth Amendment, *see Gitlow* v. *New York,* 268 U.S. 652, 672 (1925).

[37] *See Lochner* v. *New York,* 198 U.S. 45, 74, 75–76 (1905).

interference with "natural rights" of individuals. For Holmes, freedom for positive local self-government was real: [38]

> We fear to grant power and are unwilling to recognize it when it exists. . . . when legislatures are held to be authorized to do anything considerably affecting public welfare it is covered by apologetic phrases like the police power, or the statement that the business concerned has been dedicated to a public use. . . . But police power is often used in a wide sense to cover and, as I said, to apologize for the general power of the legislature to make a part of the community uncomfortable by a change.
>
> I do not believe in such apologies. I think the proper course is to recognize that a state legislature can do whatever it sees fit to do unless it is restrained by some express prohibition in the Constitution of the United States or of the State, and the Courts should be careful not to extend such prohibitions beyond their obvious meaning by reading into them conceptions of public policy that the particular Court may happen to entertain. . . . The truth seems to me to be that, subject to compensation when compensation is due, the legislature may forbid or restrict any business when it has a sufficient force of public opinion behind it.

Unlike some who came before and after him, Holmes would not restrict Due Process to its orthodox procedural context. He may have thought it futile to attempt so lost a cause. For whatever reason, the Justice confined his efforts to the more feasible task of objectifying and broadening the standards of substantive Due Process. Divorcing it from the accident of judges' economic predilection, he would fill its inherent "void" with content especially befitting a polity grounded on the total thinking processes of society. The Constitution was "made for people of fundamentally differing views." It guaranteed free expression of those views to facilitate formation of an informed consensus of opinion as the basis of government. When most members of the community after free discussion were in agreement upon the need for economic regulation, who were judges to interpose an impoverished Due Process prohibition? Holmes would limit judicial interference in such cases to those rare instances when the democratic process of discussion

[38] *See Tyson* v. *Banton,* 273 U.S. 418, 445–446 (1927). For a "compensation when compensation is due" opinion by Holmes, see *Pennsylvania Coal Co.* v. *Mahon,* 260 U.S. 393 (1922).

and consensus had so misfired as to produce results that no reasonable man could support: [39]

> I think that . . . the [Due Process Clause of the] Fourteenth Amendment is perverted when it is held to prevent the natural outcome of a dominant opinion, unless it can be said that a rational and fair man necessarily would admit that the statute proposed would infringe fundamental principles as they have been understood by the traditions of our people and our law. It does not need research to show that no such sweeping condemnation can be passed upon the [maximum hour for bakers] statute before us. A reasonable man might think it a proper measure on the score of health. Men whom I certainly could not pronounce unreasonable would uphold it as a first installment of a general regulation of the hours of work.

If to a layman the reasonable-man standard appears as slippery as judicial predilection, it is not so in the ancient tradition of the common law of which Holmes was master. Recognizing that judicial review was an established part of our constitutional system, the Justice knew all too well its tendency to degenerate into judicial supremacy. And so, to respect the one and guard against the other, he resorted to that tried and true principle of the common law which protects jury findings from intrusion by judges. Thus a legislative determination of economic relationships must stand as against Due Process objections regardless of how erroneous it may seem to judges, unless they are prepared to hold that no reasonable person could have found as the legislature did find. Holmes equated the two great institutions of an ancient heritage of freedom. For him jury and legislature—the authentic voices of the people—have the same fundamental sanctity, the same substantial independence of judicial fiat. As the Justice's leading disciple put it,[40] "In the day-to-day working of our democracy it is vital that the power of the non-democratic organ of our government be exercised with vigorous self-restraint." Just as it is a basic function of juries to temper general law with concrete justice as understood by the community, so it is a function of legislatures to conserve the Constitution by keeping it alive to popular aspirations.

[39] See note 37 *supra.*

[40] *See* Mr. Justice Frankfurter in *A. F. of L.* v. *American Sash & Door Co.,* 335 U.S. 538, 542, 555 (1949).

Of course, Due Process was not the only chink through which pseudo-laissez-faire crept into the Constitution. The division of powers between nation and states was also susceptible to interpretation in ways thoroughly compatible with the view that businessmen should have special immunity from both congressional and local regulation. Thus when Congress sought to discourage the use of child labor by excluding its products from the channels of interstate commerce, five members of the Supreme Court held that to be an undue interference with States' rights.[41] Here was a reversal of the Tenth Amendment, an expression of the concept that has been called dual federalism. For, in effect, the Court was saying that the reserved powers of the states limit the *expressly delegated* powers of the nation. The Constitution provides the exact opposite. Mr. Justice Holmes, with three associates, dissented: [42]

> The act does not meddle with anything belonging to the States. They regulate their internal affairs and their domestic commerce as they like. But when they seek to send their products across the state line they are no longer within their rights. If there were no Constitution and no Congress their power to cross the line would depend upon their neighbors. Under the Constitution such commerce belongs not to the States but to Congress to regulate. It may carry out its views of public policy whatever indirect effect they may have upon the activities of the States. Instead of being encountered by a prohibitive tariff at her boundaries the State encounters the public policy of the United States which it is for Congress to express. If, as has been the case within the memory of men still living, a State should take a different view of the propriety of sustaining a lottery from that which generally prevails, I cannot believe that the fact would require a different decision from that reached in *Champion v. Ames.* Yet in that case [as re the tariff] it would be said with quite as much force as in this that Congress was attempting to intermeddle with the State's domestic affairs. The national welfare as understood by Congress may require a different attitude within its sphere from that of some self-seeking State. It seems to me entirely constitutional for Congress to enforce its understanding by all means at its command.

To be sure, when the national tariff came before the Court,[43]

[41] *Hammer* v. *Dagenhart,* 247 U.S. 251 (1918).
[42] *Id.* at 281.
[43] *University of Illinois* v. *United States,* 288 U.S. 48 (1933); *Hampton* v. *United States,* 276 U.S. 394 (1928).

its validity was sustained, though, of course, it "meddled" with state affairs quite as much as did restrictions on the shipment of child-made goods. Thus "laissez-faire" on the bench accurately reflected the ambivalence of businessmen. For as Bryce had observed, "one-half of the capitalists are occupied in preaching laissez-faire as regards railroad control [or labor legislation], the other in resisting it—in tariff matters. . . ."

But if Holmes' Court took a dim view of national power when Congress sought to regulate business,[44] its views on that subject were generous where such an attitude served to invalidate *state* economic controls. Thus when Pennsylvania undertook to prevent fraud in the local sale of steamship tickets, the Court found "direct" interference with the dormant commerce power of Congress.[45] Holmes, Brandeis, and Stone objected: [46]

> The statute is an exertion of the police power of the state. Its evident purpose is to prevent a particular species of fraud. . . .
>
> The statute is not an obstruction of commerce. It does not discriminate against foreign commerce. It does not affect the commerce except indirectly. Congress could, of course, deal with the subject, because it is connected with foreign commerce. But it has not done so. . . . Thus there can be no contention that Congress has occupied the field. And obviously, also, this is not a case in which the silence of Congress can be interpreted as a prohibition of state action. . . . If Pennsylvania must submit to seeing its citizens defrauded, it is not because Congress has so willed, but because the Constitution so commands. [We] . . . cannot believe that it does. . . .
>
> In this case the traditional test of the limit of state action by inquiring whether the interference with commerce is direct or indirect seems . . . [to us] too mechanical, too uncertain in its application, and too remote from actualities, to be of value. In thus making use of the ex-

[44] In *Swift and Co.* v. *United States,* 196 U.S. 375 (1905) a unanimous bench went along with Holmes in the most generous view of the national power to regulate business that the Court had ever taken. One suspects that some of the "laissez-faire" Justices must have felt compelled to do so for political reasons. The legislation in question was designed to protect farmers from sharp business practices at the stockyards. It would not have been politic to antagonize both farmers and workingmen. The *Lochner* case was decided during the same year. *Adair* v. *United States,* 208 U.S. 161 (1908) was soon to come. Both were bitter blows to labor.

[45] *Di Santo* v. *Pennsylvania,* 273 U.S. 34 (1927).

[46] *Ibid.*

pressions, "direct" and "indirect interference" with commerce, we are doing little more than using labels to describe a result rather than any trustworthy formula by which it is reached.

But it is not to be supposed that Holmes was insensitive to the danger of the Balkanization of America through state interference with national affairs—nor that, like Chief Justice Taney,[47] he would leave such problems for adjustment by Congress. In a well-known paragraph he expressed his conception of the federal (as distinct from the Due Process) limits on state activity: [48]

> I do not think the United States would come to an end if we lost our power to declare an Act of Congress void. I do think the Union would be imperiled if we could not make that declaration as to the laws of the several States. For one in my place sees how often a local policy prevails with those who are not trained to national views and how often action is taken that embodies what the Commerce Clause was meant to end.

"Experiments that an important part of the community desires, in the insulated chambers afforded by the several States" [49] were one thing for Holmes; poaching on the national preserve was something else. That distinction is clear. But, initially at least, it is startling to find the Justice, normally so deferential to legislative processes, silently dissenting in *Clark Distilling Co.* v. *Western Maryland Railway*.[50] For there unbelievably the Court upheld Congressional power to override a judicial finding as to what constitutes undue local impediments on national commerce. How Congress can authorize what the Court has found to be constitutionally prohibited is a problem which the Court's opinion does not fully explain, and which to this day, though accepted,[51] has not been elucidated from the bench. The *tour de force* presumably was too much for Holmes.

Such in brief outline was the jurisprudence of Mr. Justice Holmes. Its bedrock foundation was humility and skepticism. One's

[47] *The License Cases*, 5 How. 504, 579 (1847).

[48] Holmes, *Law and the Court* in Collected Legal Papers (New York, Harcourt, Brace, 1920), pp. 295–296.

[49] *See Truax* v. *Corrigan*, 257 U.S. 312, 342–343 (1921).

[50] 242 U.S. 311 (1917).

[51] *Prudential Life Ins. Co.* v. *Benjamin*, 328 U.S. 408 (1946). See Chap. VI, below.

private beliefs are not necessarily the final truth. Certitude is not the test of truth. Accordingly, the Justice stood for free trade in ideas and the sanctity of economic legislation which embodied those thoughts that prevailed in the competition of the open market. Recognizing that all ideas are an incitement, that many are "dangerous" to the status quo, he would outlaw only those which in a given context threaten danger so immediately as to prevent the normal curative process of competition with others. Recognizing, too, that judicial review was an accepted part of our constitutional system, he was deeply aware of its abuse by his associates on the bench. And so he would restrict it (unless the Constitutional text was clear) to cases in which democracy had so misfired as to produce legislation that no reasonable person could support. Finally, the duality of a federal system induced his willingness to referee when a part interfered with the whole, that is, when a state experiment spilled over the bounds of its insulated chamber and impinged upon supra-state interests which belong to the entire people as a national unit. All of Holmes' emphasis was upon freedom to dream, to experiment and to grow. Thoroughly grounded in the history of the common law, he had learned its great lesson well —only those institutions may hope for prosperous survival which accommodate the good sense and aspirations of the people.

As the age of Victoria came to an end, Holmes, John Dewey, Thorstein Veblen, Charles Beard, and James Harvey Robinson led a pragmatic revolt against formalism, abstraction and deductive methodology in the social sciences. They would wipe out the remnants of conceptualism and syllogistic reasoning by emphasizing that "the life of science, economics and law was not logic but experience. . . ." Dewey would free philosophy of metaphysics and dedicate it to social engineering. Veblen undercut the foundations of classical economics. "Robinson was an ally in the humanization of society and knowledge; Beard punctured myths about legal institutions which blocked social change; and Holmes recognized the legislative power of judges and challenged the view that law was a deduction from divinely ordained principles of ethics." [52] What they had in common positively was a deep appreciation for the inductive methods of modern science, and the non-Euclidian

[52] Morton G. White, *Social Thought in America; The Revolt Against Formalism* (New York, Viking, 1949), pp. 11, 238.

impact of history, economics, and cultural environment upon human institutions and ideas. Working for the most part independently of one another, they were on occasion unwilling to accept each other's conclusions.[53] It was not so much the logical coherence of their respective views that gave them victory—it was rather the manner in which their common approach promised freedom from the tyranny of anachronistic dogma and the rise of a more rational society. Having carried most of the field in the years prior to World War II, their accomplishments now seem commonplace. Indeed many have forgotten (a few have rejoiced in) the strictures against which Holmes and the others fulminated. And so it happens that now in the context of different problems we hear an occasional potshot at the things for which they stood.

What critics of the pragmatic revolt particularly resent is its positivism—its insistence that morality is not less moral, nor law less legal, for being the product of a human community right here on earth. Such criticism is based on the concept of an absolute—Natural Law—to which human moral and legal systems must conform at their peril. In short, only that ethics is truly binding which springs from some transcendentally "natural" workshop. As a matter of history, he who takes this position finds it necessary to recognize some authoritarian *human agency*—if only himself—to "interpret" his supermundane codes and characteristically deals somewhat sharply with dissenters. For it is the fate of closed systems of thought to be plagued with "heretics."

The current attacks upon pragmatism in the social sciences recall the struggle of the physical sciences not so long ago to free themselves from the "eternal truths" of Aristotle and the confines of deductive reasoning. They are true to the tradition which runs from the condemnation of Socrates and the banishment of Galileo, down through the "anti-evolution" laws and the Monkey Trial, to the recent censoring of Albert Einstein as "an old faker." It is important to notice that Holmes' hecklers do not ground themselves on anything like the old Roman *jus gentium* form of natural law—an inductively derived and pragmatically tested common denominator of a host of different earthly cultures. Theirs, rather, is a "brooding omnipresence in the sky," a metaphysical construct re-

[53] Thus, for example, Veblen notwithstanding, Holmes accepted the major tenets of classical economics.

flecting, one supects, the very parochial needs of a disintegrating thirteenth century European culture. Since then it has meant all things to all men, which raises serious difficulties for those who fear that variation proves subjectivity.

Certainly in the confusing ideological conflicts of the cold war era, as in the troubled days of Aquinas, efforts to find comfort in an absolute compel sympathy.[54] But can there be more in our absolutes than human fear and frustration put into them? Is there anything in the difference between "is" and "ought" than the familiar phenomena called cultural lag—yesterday's winged "ought" being the slovenly "is" of today and so on ad infinitum? In any case, surely "oughts" are the concern of law-making (legislative), not law-enforcing (courts), branches of government. Otherwise the "independence" of judges would be an affront to the basic principle of democratic self-government.

One of the recent potshots at pragmatism is the attack upon Holmes by Mr. Harold R. McKinnon of the San Francisco Bar.[55] So thoroughly sound was the Justice in the context of his times that even Mr. McKinnon recognizes Holmes' "judicial work" was "right," insisting only that his "legal theory" was "wrong."[56] It follows that a majority of the great dissenter's associates made "wrong" decisions though by Mr. McKinnon's standards they had the "right" philosophy.

Having demolished the infidel Holmes, Mr. McKinnon might profitably turn his attention to the true believers who sat with Holmes—those faithful advocates of Natural Law who differ with Mr. McKinnon on its meaning. Whose reading is it to be, Mr.

[54] A constantly repeated theme in the attack upon Holmes appears to be that pragmatism offers no comfort or consolation. See William L. Lucey, *Holmes—Liberal—Humanitarian—Believer in Democracy?*, 39 Geo. L. J. 523, 528, 529, 536, 538 especially, 555–557 (1951). But does the validity of a philosophy depend upon its ability to comfort or console? If Father Lucey thinks so, he is far more of a pragmatist than he purports to be. Reversing Hobbes, he apparently bases his natural law system on a pragmatic foundation.

[55] See McKinnon, *The Secret of Mr. Justice Holmes,* 36 A. B. A. J. 261 (1950). See also Palmer, *Hobbes, Holmes and Hitler,* 31 A. B. A. J. 569 (1945); William L. Lucey, *Natural Law and American Legal Realism,* 30 Geo. L. J. 493 (1942); J. C. Ford, *The Fundamentals of Holmes' Juristic Philosophy* in Clarence E. Sloane, Phases of American Culture (Worcester, Holy Cross, 1942), p. 51.

[56] McKinnon, *supra* note 55, at 345. See also 343, 344.

Justice Sutherland's, Mr. McKinnon's or John Doe's? A democrat might answer, "That which prevails in the competition of a free intellectual market, in other words, what most people in the community will accept as just after opportunity for the intellectual cross-fertilization that comes with free discussion." But Mr. McKinnon seems to have little but contempt for the ethical views of "the people." [57] The alternatives, of course, are anarchy or authoritarianism. It seems never to have occurred to our critic that both the people and their political representatives might have natural law insights—that judges do not necessarily have an exclusive monopoly in that realm. Indeed, if one insists upon medieval terminology, it may be said that Holmes' genius consists precisely in his attacks upon the judicial monopolization of natural law. For if the Justice's words are read in the context of time and place, it is clear that they were directed not so much against natural law as against the judicial perversion of it.

To leap word-fences and come to grips with the reality that lies behind them is a lesson that young Oliver must have learned in the revolt which his father and "Uncle Waldo" Emerson led against the New England perversion of puritanism. The difficulty is that the great concept of natural law may be, and on the bench as elsewhere often has been, perverted into an elastic formulary to sugarcoat a narrow and sometimes selfish parochialism. It is one thing to press natural law against a king who purports to rule by divine right; to urge it in conjunction with judicial supremacy [58] to frustrate democratic self-government is something quite different. To urge one's personal absolute as a norm against which to *discuss* earthly justice is quite different from insisting upon it as the only true and binding ethics. Finally, we may accept the idea of natural law without adopting the view that it is somehow "natural" only to judges and not to voters or their political representatives.

For Mr. Justice Holmes morality was not less moral for being the product of the human community in which he lived. He did not require the occult to bolster his sense of decency, not to justify his faith in the perfectibility of man. He preferred to formulate his major premises not from preconceptions, but from experience and

[57] *Id.* at 264, 343, 345.

[58] I use the term as Attorney General (now Mr. Justice) Jackson used it in his, The Struggle for Judicial Supremacy (New York, Knopf, 1941).

observation. True to the democratic tradition, he honored the inquiring mind—for him there were no heretics. His skepticism was in the ancient Greek tradition that questioning is the road to knowledge. He "had the moral courage to accept uncertainty and the intellectual humility to know that he could not know—This is Truth." [59]

[59] See Fred Rodell, *Justice Holmes and His Hecklers,* 60 Yale Law Journal 620 (1951).

VI

JUSTICES BLACK AND FRANKFURTER

The New Court and the New Freedom

Nothing perhaps since the Civil War has made so deep a mark upon America as the Great Depression. Stimulated by the Gospel of Wealth, business had all but solved the world's oldest problem: shortage of the necessities and amenities of life. Yet ultimately this neo-Hamiltonianism failed. Preoccupied with production for pecuniary gain, it neglected the problem of distribution. More accurately, perhaps, its opulence created that problem. Distributive techniques inherited from ages of poverty were inadequate for an era of mass production. As Brooks Adams saw it, the industrial revolution had "evolved under the stress of an environment which demanded excessive specialization in . . . money-making. . . . To this money-making attribute all else had been sacrificed. . . ." [1]

Despite "artificial" restraints on production which Veblen lampooned in the *Engineers and the Price System,* goods piled up periodically beyond the market's ability to absorb. In this some economists found the nub of the business cycle of feast and famine. In any case, when the old order collapsed in the Great Depression, its stoutest defenders found the fault in "overproduction"—in a world of want and hunger. Brooks Adams no doubt would have blamed over-specialization. The modern Keynesian explanation is

[1] Quoted in Ralph H. Gabriel, *The Course of American Democratic Thought,* 2nd ed. (New York, Ronald 1956), p. 243.

"over-saving"—a choking accumulation of funds which found no outlet either in consumption or production. This idle money meant idle markets and idle men. Under earlier mass-poverty conditions it may have been a safe assumption that savings automatically became productive capital. Experience in an opulent, mass-manufacturing economy taught a different lesson. Businessmen were not inclined to expand plant capacity in the face of "overproduction." Their idle savings went into speculation on the stock market and in real estate—with a resulting "boom and bust" that ushered in the Great Depression.

The impact of economic disaster revitalized the political party system, which is to say simply that it accelerated the shift to what A. N. Holcombe in 1933 called "the new party politics": [2]

> The passing of the frontier and the growth of urban industry have shaken the foundations of the old party system in national politics. The old sectional interests are changing and the old sectional alliances are breaking down. The old party politics is visibly passing away. The character of the new party politics will be determined chiefly by the interests and attitudes of the urban population. It will be less rustic than the old and more urbane. There will be less sectional and more class politics.

Industrialization had transformed America into a nation of city-dwellers. Labor had replaced the farmer as the *bête noire* of businessmen. Industry, throttled by the institutions of an earlier economy of scarcity, could not distribute the plentiful fruits of mass production. The Common Man faced starvation in the midst of plenty. These new horizontal fissures in American life began to rival the old vertical tensions of sectionalism at the core of national politics. Only the catalyzing magic of a new political leader was wanting.

When the national economy collapsed, Franklin Roosevelt succeeded where Bryan had failed. As Samuel Lubell explained: [3]

> The really revolutionary surge behind the New Deal lay in this coupling of the depression with the rise of a new generation, which had been mal-nourished on the congestion of our cities and the abuses of

[2] Arthur N. Holcombe, *The New Party Politics* (New York, Norton, 1933), p. 11.

[3] *The Future of American Politics* (London, Hamish Hamilton, 1952), pp. 29, 50.

industrialism. Roosevelt did not start this revolt of the city. What he did do was to waken the climbing urban masses to a consciousness of the power in their numbers. . . . In turn, the big-city masses furnished the votes which re-elected Roosevelt again and again—and, in the process, ended the traditional Republican [sectional] majority in this country. . . . In the past American political realignments have always followed sectional lines. The Revolt of the City, however, has drawn the same class-conscious line of economic interest across the entire country, overriding not only regional distinctions but equally strong cultural differences.

The New Deal "revolution" and much that followed was an experiment in the problem of distribution—of finding ways for the Common Man to acquire the vast goods which industry knew how to produce.[4] Madison Avenue and installment credit for consumers had not sufficed.

What position would the Supreme Court take in the face of the nation's broad new legislative program? Could judicial review continue to dominate national policy? With boldness reminiscent of its counter-revolution in the 1890's, the old Court struck down virtually the whole New Deal recovery program.[5] Indeed, it went so far that Mr. Justice Cardozo is said to have remarked, "We are no longer a Court." But what judges had achieved—or had thrust upon them—under a petrified sectionalism, they could not maintain in the face of a vigorous, new urban politics. Like the great statesmen of the old politics of sections (Jefferson, Jackson and Lincoln), the first master of urban politics had his way with the Court. The "Packing Plan" of 1937, like the Chase impeachment of 1805, failed only in its immediate implications. Saving face as best it could, the old Court immediately retreated.[6] Within three years most of the "nine old men" had left the bench. It is worth passing notice that the four arch-conservatives of the old judicial regime

[4] For example, the Social Security Act, the National Labor Relations Act, the Agricultural Adjustment Acts, the Fair Labor Standards Act which were calculated to increase the purchasing power of labor, farmers, the aged, the handicapped and the unemployed. The Reciprocal Trade Agreements Act was designed to restore our foreign markets.

[5] See, for example, *United States* v. *Butler,* 297 U.S. 1 (1936); *Schechter* v. *United States,* 295 U.S. 495 (1935); *Carter* v. *Carter Coal Co.,* 298 U.S. 238 (1936).

[6] The major turning point seems to have been *NLRB* v. *Jones & Laughlin Steel Co.,* 301 U.S. 1 (1937).

had been reared in the post-bellum frontier atmosphere of Utah (Sutherland), Wyoming (Van Deventer), Tennessee (McReynolds) and Minnesota (Butler)—while their four great liberal contemporaries (Holmes, Brandeis, Stone and Cardozo) made their mark in huge urban centers in Massachusetts and New York. The passing of the frontier and the transition from sectional to urban politics seems to have had at least symbolic repercussions on the bench.

Whatever may be said about disagreement within the new Court, on one major point there has been *complete unanimity:* "laissez-faire" is not a mandate of the Constitution. Its legal vehicles—Dual Federalism and the old Substantive Due Process—have been discarded. The new wine which Mr. Justice Field worked so hard to put into the ancient vessel of Due Process has been removed.[7] Waite's admonition again prevails: for removal of economic legislation deemed unwise, the remedy is the polls, not the courts. Federal powers, no longer impeded by an "invisible radiation from the Tenth Amendment," have regained the status which Marshall recognized: [8]

> The wisdom and discretion of Congress, their identity with the people, and the influence which their constituents possess at elections, are in [the regulation of interstate commerce], as in many other instances, as that, for example of declaring war, the sole restraints on which they have relied, to secure them from its abuse.

In short, the American people are free again to choose their own economic policies without judicial interference. This "return to the Constitution" entails more, however, than abandonment of pseudo-laissez-faire. It is part of the Jeffersonian tradition, handed down through Taney, Waite, and Holmes among others. The new Court has vetoed congressional measures only to protect civil liberty.[9]

[7] See for example, *Lincoln Federal Labor Union* v. *Northwestern Iron Co.,* 335 U.S. 525 (1949).

[8] *Gibbons* v. *Ogden,* 9 Wheaton 1 (1824) and see *United States* v. *Darby Lumber Co.,* 312 U.S. 100 (1941).

[9] More specifically it has struck down, or limited the application of, federal legislation only in the interest of fair trials. *Tot* v. *United States,* 319 U.S. 463 (1943); *United States* v. *Lovett,* 328 U.S. 303 (1946); *United States* v. *Cardiff,* 344 U.S. 174 (1952); *United States* v. *Toth,* 350 U.S. 11 (1955); *Reid* v. *Covert,* 354 U.S. 1 (1957); *Trop* v. *Dulles,* 356 U.S. 86 (1958). In this area alone apparently the Court has deemed itself to have a special competence and responsibility vis-à-vis the national legislature.

With minor exceptions,[10] it has invalidated state legislature only to safeguard civil liberty, or to prevent a state from interfering with national interests. Judges deeply respectful of democracy hesitate to intrude upon the political processes, except to protect the most basic human freedoms or to resolve conflicts in the partial interregnum between our 51 state and national democratic systems. This is the essence of the new constitutional law.

On the rejection of "laissez-faire" the new judges have been in *constant* and *complete* agreement. Their much advertised differences are confined to the limited area of civil liberty and federalism. More particularly, the issue has been this: how far shall a court go in overriding the political processes for the protection of personal freedom; how far in preventing a state from poaching upon the national preserve? Or conversely, to what extent should such matters be left for solution by the political processes themselves? On these issues the Court, like the rest of us, is deeply divided. Justices Black and Frankfurter appear to be the chief spokesmen for opposing views.

FEDERALISM

One of the great flaws of the Articles of Confederation was the sovereign freedom of each state to pursue its own ends at whatever cost to its sister states and the general welfare. Indeed, state trade barriers were a major reason for the calling of the Constitutional Convention. As Madison put it, the "practice of many States in restricting the commercial intercourse with other States . . . is certainly adverse to the spirit of the Union, and tends to beget retaliatory regulations . . . destructive of the general harmony." The Virginia Plan, which Randolph presented to the Constitutional Convention, proposed "that the National Legislature ought to be empowered . . . to negative all laws passed by the several States contravening in the opinion of the National Legislature the articles of Union. . . ." In part this principle is embedded in the Constitution. For example, the states are forbidden "without the consent of Congress" to lay imposts or duties on foreign trade (Article I, Sec. 10). The New Jersey Plan, on the other hand, relied upon

[10] See *Wood* v. *Lovett*, 313 U.S. 362 (1941); *Morey* v. *Doud*, 354 U.S. 457 (1957).

national military power to keep the states from interfering with the general welfare. This perhaps is reflected in the constitutional provision which requires the President to "take care that the [federal] laws be faithfully executed. . . ." (Article II, Sec. 3). But for ordinary cases of state recalcitrance, both Virginia's political, and New Jersey's military—or executive—approach were rejected. The Founding Fathers chose instead judicial mediation. This finds expression in the mandate that national law—Constitution, statutes and treaties—shall be "the supreme law of the land . . . any thing in the constitution or laws of any state to the contrary notwithstanding" (Article VI, Par. 2). This, of course, is the foundation of the Supreme Court's authority to safeguard the whole from the selfishness of its parts. As Madison put it, ". . . the Federal Judiciary is truly the only defensive armor of the Federal Government, or rather for the Constitution and laws of the United States. Strip it of that armor, and the door is wide open for nullification, anarchy and convulsion. . . ."[11]

Part of the supreme law, of course, is that Congress shall have power to "regulate commerce among the several states" (Article I, Sec. 8). The most persistent and most litigated problem in constitutional law is this: when Congress has not exercised its commerce power in a manner which precludes state action, to what extent are the states free to tax and regulate interstate trade? Marshall, it will be recalled, apparently preferred the view that the commerce power is exclusively national. It followed that whether or not Congress had acted, the states could not tax o regulate commerce among the several states. Taney's view wa just the opposite: the states are free to act in the absence of con flicting national legislation. A "compromise" was reached whe *Cooley* v. *Board of Wardens*[12] recognized that there are differer kinds of interstate commerce, "some imperatively demanding single uniform rule . . . ; and some . . . as imperatively demand ing that diversity [of treatment], which alone can meet the loc necessities. . . ." Thus in the one category the commerce pow was exclusively national; in the other it was concurrent, i.e., su

[11] Quoted in Charles Warren, *The Supreme Court in United Sta History* (Boston, Little Brown, 1937), Vol. 1, p. 740.

[12] 12 Howard 299 (1851).

ject to state control in the absence of incompatible federal legislation.

The *Cooley* compromise and its off-shoots [13] became orthodox law, but, like Due Process and the Tenth Amendment, they succumbed to "laissez-faire." They became vehicles for imposing the Gospel of Wealth upon the states.[14] Of course, this perversion has been dropped by the New Court. But Mr. Justice Black goes further. He would revive Taney's view, which in effect makes Congress the sole judge of the extent to which states may deal with interstate commerce.[15] The late Mr. Justice Jackson would have gone a large part of the way back to Marshall. Experience under the Articles of Confederation demonstrated for all time the fate of a nation without an effective shield from parochial selfishness. The subsequent history of state efforts to secure local advantage at national expense makes the old lesson ever new. Usually, "these restraints are individually too petty, too diversified, and too local to get the attention of a Congress hard pressed with more urgent matters. The practical result is that in default of action [by the Court] they will go on suffocating, and retarding and Balkanizing American commerce, trade and industry." [16] It followed for Mr. Justice Jackson that Marshall's view was essentially sound: the Court must take a *very strict* view of state measures impinging upon national commerce.

Between these two extremes, Mr. Justice Frankfurter—since the death of Chief Justice Stone—has led the Court in a middle position, in the spirit of the *Cooley* compromise. To put it briefly: the states must be allowed the greatest sphere of freedom compatible with the needs of an open national market for all goods and services.[17]

Of course neither the *Cooley* rule nor its off-shoots are prescribed explicitly in the Constitution. They are judge-made. Some

[13] As to the off-shoots see Mr. Justice Black's dissenting opinion in *Hood* v. *DuMond,* 336 U.S. 525, 545 (1949).

[14] See, for example, *DiSanto* v. *Pennsylvania,* 273 U.S. 34 (1927).

[15] See, for example, his opinions in *Hood* v. *DuMond,* 336 U.S. 525, 551 Note 2 (1949); *Southern Pacific Co.* v. *Arizona,* 325 U.S. 761, 784 (1945); *J. D. Adams* v. *Storen,* 304 U.S. 307, 316 (1938).

[16] *Duckworth* v. *Arkansas,* 314 U.S. 390, 400 (1941).

[17] See, for example, *Freeman* v. *Hewit,* 329 U.S. 249 (1946); *McLeod* v. *Dilworth,* 322 U.S. 327 (1944).

problems, not unlike this, as to which the Constitution provides no criteria for judgment, the Court declines to adjudicate. Under the doctrine of "political questions" it refers them for settlement to the elective branches of government. Perhaps the paradox of supplying the *Cooley* standards in the commerce area and refusing to furnish standards elsewhere has burdened the conscience of judges recently much preoccupied with the sanctity of democratic government. They have not gone so far as to abandon jurisdiction to save the national market from local burdens. After all, ". . . Congress has accommodated its legislation, as have the states, to these [judge-made] rules as an established feature of our constitutional system."[18] And so perhaps to reconcile an ancient accepted tradition with a sharpened sensitivity to the demands of democracy, the Court now recognizes congressional power to override its application of the *Cooley* principle. Congress "may either permit the states to regulate the commerce in a manner which would otherwise not be permissible or exclude state regulation even of matters of peculiarly local concern which nevertheless affect interstate commerce."[19] This is not entirely new, for on a few earlier occasions the Court has permitted itself to be overruled by Congress in such matters.[20] But what was generally considered a rare anomaly has now become the law of the land.[21]

The democratic philosophy behind the new Court's position is plain. What Congress does is subject to the political consent of *all the people*. But what a state does, though it may affect the whole nation, carries the consent of only *a few of the people*. We did not trust the welfare of the whole to any of its parts. This, of course, is the meaning of the Supremacy Clause itself. A similar thought finds expression in Madison's famous argument in *The Federalist*, No. 10. The smaller the political entity, the easier it is for a petty, parochial interest to prevail. The wider the political circle and the more numerous the clashing selfish interests, the more surely will they cancel each other out in favor of a common denominator: the general welfare. Judicial veto of an act of Congress defies this

[18] *Southern Pacific Co.* v. *Arizona*, 325 U.S. 761, 770 (1945).

[19] *Id.* p. 769.

[20] See, for example, the *Wheeling Bridge* case discussed in Chap. III, above.

[21] *Prudential Insurance Co.* v. *Benjamin*, 328 U.S. 408 (1946).

safety-in-number principle. But when the Court blocks local intrusion upon the national domain, it merely maintains an open field for the free play of the whole political process.

CIVIL LIBERTY—THE FAIR TRIAL IN STATE CRIMINAL CASES

Possibly the most troublesome provision in the Constitution is the Due Process Clause of the Fourteenth Amendment. Linguistically and historically, Due Process is a procedural admonition calculated to insure fair trials. Obviously such a concept cannot be formulated in a neat catch-all rule of thumb. Yet Judge Learned Hand seems to have caught its essence when he said that it embodies the English sporting sense of fair play. Obviously this at best is broad, even when confined within its orthodox procedural bounds. When the old Court stretched it wider to cover substantive economic interests, Mr. Justice Holmes observed that only the sky was the limit. Of course, the new judges have been unanimous in draining Due Process of its improvised "laissez-faire" content. But there is still difficulty as to its proper scope.

Mr. Justice Black's solution is heroic. He insists that Due Process (and related clauses in the Fourteenth Amendment, "separately and as a whole") mean no more and no less as a restraint upon state action, than the Bill of Rights means as a restraint upon the national government.[22] Indeed, he insists, that was the avowed purpose of the Fourteenth Amendment. In this manner the Justice would give the vague provisions of the Civil War amendment a more "precise" content—and thereby forestall repetition of the old "laissez-faire" or similar abuse.

Mr. Justice Frankfurter, constantly preoccupied with the Constitution as a living instrument of government, cannot join his brother's retreat into the eighteenth century. He cannot accept the idea that the Anglo-American concept of procedural fairness meant no more in 1868 when the Fourteenth Amendment was adopted, than it meant in 1791 when the Bill of Rights became law. Nor can he believe that the growth of our understanding of fairness in trial procedure ended in 1791 or 1868. But the "short answer" to the suggestion that Due Process means what the Bill of Rights means

[22] *Adamson* v. *California,* 332 U.S. 46, 71–2 (1949).

is that this is a strange way of saying so. Moreover, it would seem "too late in the day to [argue] that a phrase so laden with historic meaning . . . can be given an improvised content. . . ."[23]—particularly when to do so either gets its author nowhere—for he has simply incorporated the Due Process Clause of the Fifth Amendment into the Fourteenth—or forces him to find new meaning in the former, or none at all. For Mr. Justice Frankfurter the guideposts are nothing less than "those canons of decency and fairness which express the notions of justice of English-speaking people."[24] Essentially what is involved is a "judgment that reflects deep, even if inarticulate, feelings of our society. Judges must devine that feeling as best they can from all the relevant evidence and light which they can bring to bear. . . ." Then he adds parenthetically, "It is noteworthy that while American experience has been drawn upon in the framing of constitutions for other democratic countries, the Due Process Clause has not been copied."[25] He put it more emphatically before he came to the bench; "The due process clauses ought to go."[26] But they have not gone, and on the bench such private views are out of place. "These are very broad terms by which to accommodate freedom and authority. As has been suggested from time to time, they may be too large to serve as the basis for adjudication, in that they allow much room for individual notions of policy. . . . The fact is that the duty of adjudication on a basis no less narrow has been committed to this Court."[27]

There is another—a federalistic—dimension to the problem. Whatever its content, the Fourteenth Amendment is a restraint upon States' rights—and states' *responsibilities.* The broader its content, the less that is left to local self-government *in local affairs.* The narrower its content, the narrower the federal shield for the individual. Obviously Justices Black and Frankfurter agree that Due Process is less precise than constitutional provisions ought to be. In seeking standards for guidance in its application, they disagree as to where the balance should be struck between past and present, between States rights and individual interests, between

[23] *Id.* 63; *Malinski* v. *New York,* 324 U.S. 401, 416 (1945).
[24] *Id.* 417.
[25] *Haley* v. *Ohio,* 332 U.S. 569, 603 (1948).
[26] "The Red Terror of Judicial Reform," *New Republic,* Oct. 1, 1924.
[27] *Louisiana ex rel. Francis* v. *Resweber,* 329 U.S. 459, 468 (1947).

the role of the courts and the role of the people in giving content to the American dream of individual freedom and local self-government.

Mr. Justice Frankfurter's position is orthodox. Apart from the "laissez-faire" fiasco, it has been followed by the Court from the beginning.[28] If Mr. Justice Black's attack is broad, in practice the difference in the two views seems to center largely on "the right to counsel." Must a state furnish lawyers for indigent defendants in criminal cases? This narrow but important point at which the real pinch comes illustrates the basic difference between the two judges. One is an idealist, the other a pragmatist. The Court and Mr. Justice Frankfurter will upset a state conviction on counsel grounds via the Due Process blunderbuss only on a showing that the indigent did in fact suffer for want of appointed counsel.[29] In a word, the fair conduct of state trials is essentially a state responsibility; only for actual, demonstrated unfairness is federal interference permissible.

The full import of Mr. Justice Frankfurter's position in these states cases can be grasped only when one recognizes that he is not to be outdone in strict enforcement of meticulous standards in federal criminal proceedings.[30] Clearly the Justice finds his supervisory duty with respect to lower federal courts quite different from his constitutional function vis-à-vis state judicial systems.

This cold, cerebral approach is not for Mr. Justice Black. His generous heart is ever responsive to those who excite sympathy. Dissenting, he would follow an iron rule that, regardless of any showing of fairness or unfairness, no state trial can be valid unless the accused had—or properly waived—aid of counsel.[31] But what does the Justice do in a Due Process case cursed with a modern form of unfairness not contemplated by the old eighteenth century Bill of Rights? Such was *Griffin* v. *Illinois*.[32] To preserve the eyesight of its judges, Illinois required that the record of a case on appeal be presented in printed form. But suppose a convict cannot

[28] See *Palko* v. *Connecticut*, 302 U.S. 319 (1937).

[29] *Betts* v. *Brady*, 316 U.S. 455 (1942).

[30] See, for example, *Bruno* v. *United States*, 308 U.S. 287 (1939); *McNabb* v. *United States*, 328 U.S. 463 (1946); *Harris* v. *United States*, 331 U.S. 145 (1947).

[31] *Betts* v. *Brady*, 316 U.S. 455, 474 (1942).

[32] 351 U.S. 12 (1956).

pay the high cost of printing. The Bill of Rights says not a word on the subject. Without explanation, Mr. Justice Black went along with his brother Frankfurter and the Court in seeing to it that Griffin had a fair hearing. Similarly the Bill of Rights does not explicitly outlaw convictions based on false evidence knowingly introduced, nor criminal statutes which do not adequately define what conduct is illegal, nor indeed racial discrimination. Yet in cases raising these problems, as in *Griffin's* case, Mr. Justice Black felt compelled to come out of the eighteenth century and accept Due Process—like Equal Protection—as a dynamic, living concept.[33]

On the other hand, the Bill of Rights provides for indictment by grand jury and jury trials in *all* criminal cases and in civil cases involving more than twenty dollars.[34] It is impossible to believe that, if put to the test, Mr. Justice Black would insist that these are fully imposed upon the states by the Fourteenth Amendment. Indictment by grand jury is a costly and cumbersome process inspired by social conditions that no longer exist. Even at the time the Fourteenth Amendment was adopted almost half of the ratifying states had abandoned the rigorous, old indictment system. Today more than half the states have done so. For minor offenses at the state and local level, the petit jury has been all but obsolete in most states for generations. It is not to be forgotten that the requirement of jury trials in *all* federal prosecutions was adopted on the understanding that there were relatively few federal—as against state—crimes and what there were were generally weighty. This remains true. To insist upon trial by jury for *all* petty state and local offenses would be as great a perversion as to insist upon juries in all state civil cases involving more than twenty dollars. Twenty dollars was one thing in 1791; it is something very different now. Indeed, by act of Congress, federal trial courts, except in special circumstances, do not even have jurisdiction to hear a civil case involving less than ten thousand dollars.

Just as Mr. Justice Black on occasion goes beyond his *Adamson* rule, so perhaps in practice he would not insist upon full "incorporation" of the indictment and jury provisions. Apart from these the

[33] *Alcorta* v. *Texas,* 355 U.S. 28 (1947); *Winters* v. *New York,* 333 U.S. 507 (1948); *Brown* v. *Topeka,* 347 U.S. 483 (1954).

[34] See Fifth, Sixth and Seventh Amendments.

"new" Court has neither found, nor intimated, that Due Process in the Fourteenth Amendment means less than was *originally* contemplated by the Bill of Rights. After all, the orthodox, historic meaning of the "right to counsel" provision in the Sixth Amendment was the right to *employ* counsel—not to have counsel furnished by government.[35] The Fourth Amendment doubtless meant what it says in outlawing unreasonable search and seizure—but it says nothing about the exclusion from a trial of wholely reliable, if improperly obtained, evidence.[36] Freedom from double jeopardy no doubt was meant to bar repeated trials for the same offense. It is something very different to hold that government cannot appeal a case to correct errors for the purpose of securing *one fair trial.*[37] Freedom from self-incrimination was meant to outlaw Star Chamber tactics. To prevent a prosecutor from commenting to a jury upon the failure of the accused to testify in his own defense is quite another matter.[38]

Plainly the Court has "refined" or expanded the meaning of the Bill of Rights in its application to federal prosecutions. Refusal to impose these "innovations" upon the states rests in part, of course, on federalistic considerations. It may also indicate a belief that some of them, reflecting the rugged individualism of an earlier era, are less than wise or effective now. The federal rule upsetting convictions based on reliable, if improperly obtained, evidence helps those who have something to hide. It does nothing for the innocent whose privacy has been illegally disturbed. More direct sanctions for protecting privacy—of the innocent as well as the guilty—are available for any state that wants to adopt them. To deny government a right of appeal in the interest of *one fair trial,* while allowing it to the convict, smacks of treating the public in the serious business of law enforcement on a heads-I-win-tails-you-lose basis. To deny prosecutors the power to comment to the jury on the accused's failure to "explain" the evidence against him seems unimportant. With or without such comment, men sitting as jurors are not apt to ignore the kind of inference that comes naturally in their every-day lives. Of course all persons accused of crime ought

[35] Cf. *Betts* v. *Brady,* 316 U.S. 455 (1942).
[36] Cf. *Wolf* v. *Colorado,* 338 U.S. 25 (1949).
[37] Cf. *Palko* v. *Connecticut,* 302 U.S. 319 (1937).
[38] Cf. *Adamson* v. *California,* 332 U.S. 46 (1947).

to have the assistance of counsel, but as the Department of Justice has told Congress time after time, the only effective way to get it for indigents is through legislative appropriations for counsel fees.

Meanwhile *Powell* v. *Alabama*[39] and *Betts* v. *Brady*[40] provide recourse for those who can make a reasonable showing that in fact they suffered for want of counsel. To go further with Mr. Justice Black would free some convicts who, by the efforts of prosecutors and judges, enjoyed every reasonable protection. After all, many men fully aware of their guilt plead guilty, wanting neither juries nor lawyers to prolong their agony. Then, having been fairly treated, they may undergo a change of heart—after time has assuaged the burden of their guilt. In such cases, right to counsel is an afterthought entirely unrelated to its true purpose. In short, there are many guilty men in jail who had fair trials, though they had no counsel. So too, no doubt, there are those who did not have fair trials—with or without legal representation.

Mr. Justice Black's problem is plain. Repelled by the license of the "laissez-faire" judges, he wants certainty in the law. Hence his iron-clad rule as to the meaning of the Fourteenth Amendment. But rules rigid enough to foreclose the old "laissez-faire" abuse would prevent cure of what the Justice sees as present evils. To curb judicial discretion is to curb it for good as well as for ill. Thus the judge is caught between his desire for certainty and his desire for Justice. And so in *Griffin's* case—and elsewhere—he silently and temporarily abandons his insistence that the generalities of the Fourteenth Amendment mean no more and no less than the Bill of Rights.[41] In *Zorach* v. *Clauson*[42] Mr. Justice Black ran into another impasse. Incorporation of the Bill of Rights into the Fourteenth Amendment is supposed to give the latter a precise content.[43] Yet the only two judges who fully sponsor the incorporation principle —Black and Douglas—could not agree with each other as to whether the Bill of Rights outlawed the *Zorach* release-time sys-

39 287 U.S. 45 (1932).

40 316 U.S. 455 (1942).

41 Similarly in *Morgan* v. *Virginia*, 328 U.S. 373 (1946), the Justice abandons his rule (see footnote 15 above) as to the limited restraining effect of the Commerce Clause on state regulations.

42 343 U.S. 306 (1952).

43 *FPC* v. *Natural Gas Pipeline*, 315 U.S. 575, 600 Note 4 (1942), and Mr. Justice Black's *Adamson* opinion *passim*.

tem. Nor is this the only example of their disagreement as to the meaning of the supposedly precise provisions of the Bill of Rights.[44]

Mr. Justice Frankfurter—with the Court—avoids such embarrassment. For him Due Process means a fair trial—a concept that grows with our growing experience. Discretion is inherent in constitutional adjudication because the Constitution—designed for an unknowable future—is necessarily imprecise. Precision would hamstring progress. As Dean Pound put it, the law must be stable, yet cannot stand still. Mr. Justice Frankfurter does not try to hide, or apologize for, the discretionary element in adjudication. Nor does he try to eliminate it with improvised iron rules. Rather he would exercise it humbly, not in accordance with his own heart's desire, but by the guidance of an external standard: the reasonable man. Who is this creature? He is the same old genius who made the common law one of the world's two great legal systems. He is simply a norm whereby judges, saddled with law as vague as Due Process, seek guidance in the good sense, the sober second thought, the conscience of the community—or, as the Justice put it, the "deep, even if inarticulate, feelings of our society."

CIVIL LIBERTY—THE FAIR TRIAL IN SECURITY CASES

The Cold War presents old problems of fair procedure in a new context. May government, in an administrative proceeding, bring security charges against an employee and dismiss him without an opportunity to know in detail, and refute, the evidence against him? What is the meaning of Due Process in such a setting? These problems were raised in *Bailey* v. *Richardson* [45] but because the Court was evenly divided (Mr. Justice Clark not sitting), it could give no opinion. This left intact a lower court decision that Due Process did not require a full, court-like "trial" where "mere" dismissal, as distinct from criminal penalties, were involved. But in *Joint Anti-Fascist Committee* v. *McGrath* [46] five judges (including Mr. Justice Clark) agreed that Due Process required notice and an opportunity to be heard before the Attorney General could "list"

[44] See, for example, *Ciucci* v. *Illinois*, 356 U.S. 571 (1948); *Wolf* v. *Colorado*, 338 U.S. 25 (1949); *Zorach* v. *Clauson*, 343 U.S. 306 (1952).

[45] 341 U.S. 918 (1951).

[46] 341 U.S. 123 (1951).

an organization as subversive. A sixth judge, Mr. Justice Burton, apparently found this implicit in the executive order under which the listing had been authorized. Chief Justice Vinson with Justices Reed and Minton argued in dissent that no constitutional rights were infringed by the mere designation of an organization as subversive.

Other federal cases of this type have been disposed of without reaching constitutional issues. *Communist Party* v. *Subversive Activities Control Board* [47] returned a subversive listing to the Board "to make certain that [it] bases its findings on untainted evidence." Three of the original witnesses before the Board had subsequently discredited themselves and their testimony. *Peters* v. *Hobey* [48] again raised the problem of whether a federal employee may be discharged on security grounds where the adverse findings reflected the statements of "secret" or "faceless" informers. The issue did not have to be decided since in the Court's view the Review Board had no authority to issue its order, the case not having been presented to it by a proper appeal. *Cole* v. *Young* [49] upset a summary dismissal of a federal employee because the act of Congress authorizing such dismissal was found applicable only to those in "sensitive" positions and no finding of "sensitivity" had been made in Cole's case. The discharge of a principal target of the McCarthy fury was upset in *Service* v. *Dulles*,[50] on the ground that the dismissing agency had violated its own relevant regulations. *Harmon* v. *Brucker* [51] held that the Secretary of the Army had exceeded his statutory authority by giving a less than honorable discharge based on *pre-induction* political affiliations of the dischargee. *Green* v. *McElroy* [52] held that the Department of Defense had not been authorized either by the President or by Congress to create the industrial security clearance program under which Greene had lost his position with a private manufacturer of munitions. In this case Mr. Justice Clark dissented alone. Four judges (Black, Douglas, Brennan and Stewart) found it proper to join in Chief Justice Warren's dictum that

[47] 351 U.S. 115 (1956).
[48] 349 U.S. 331 (1955).
[49] 351 U.S. 536 (1956).
[50] 354 U.S. 363 (1957).
[51] 355 U.S. 579 (1948).
[52] 79 S. Ct. 1400 (1959).

> Certain principles have remained relatively immutable in our jurisprudence. One of these is that where governmental action seriously injures an individual, and the reasonableness of the action depends on fact findings, the evidence used to prove the Government's case must be disclosed to the individual so that he has an opportunity to show that it is untrue. While this is important in the case of documentary evidence, it is even more important where the evidence consists of the testimony of individuals whose memory might be faulty or who, in fact, might be perjurers or persons motivated by malice, vindictiveness, intolerance, prejudice or jealousy. We have formalized these protections in the requirements of confrontation and cross-examination.

The related case of *Kent* v. *Dulles*[53] held that Congress had not authorized the Secretary of State to withold a passport because of the applicant's political beliefs and associations.

These decisions—only one of which was decided without dissent—are classic examples of the ancient principle that the Court will not decide constitutional issues when litigation may be settled on other grounds. This and related principles—for avoidance of major surgery when less drastic remedies are available—are summarized in Mr. Justice Brandeis' classic opinion in *Ashwander* v. *TVA*.[54] Their particular virtue in the Cold War security cases is that they have permitted protection of the individual without foreclosing congressional authority to work out appropriate ways of reconciling crucial public and private interests. It is noteworthy that in *Peters* Mr. Justice Black indicated impatience with the Court's refusal to face the constitutional issue, but only Mr. Justice Douglas thought it could not be avoided.

New York, evidently profiting from federal experience, adopted the Feinberg Law which provides for a listing of subversive organizations after notice and hearing. It also provides that a person's membership in a listed organization shall be "prima facie evidence of disqualification for appointment to or retention in" a public school position. Persons running afoul of the presumption are given an opportunity to rebut it in hearings made subject to judicial review. The measure was upheld in *Adler* v. *Bd. of Education of the City of New York:*[55]

[53] 357 U.S. 116 (1958).
[54] 297 U.S. 288 (1936).
[55] 342 U.S. 485 (1952).

A teacher works in a sensitive area in a schoolroom. There he shapes the attitude of young minds towards the society in which they live. In this, the state has a vital concern. . . . That the school authorities have the right and the duty to screen the officials, teachers, and employees as to their fitness to maintain the integrity of the schools as a part of ordered society, cannot be doubted. One's associations, past and present, as well as one's conduct, may properly be considered in determining fitness and loyalty.

Justices Black and Douglas dissented both on the substantive ground that this constituted censorship and on the procedural ground that the authorized hearings were inadequate. Mr. Justice Frankfurter dissented in the belief that the problem was not ready for adjudication (in accordance with principles listed in the Brandeis *Ashwander* opinion). The Feinberg Law had not yet gone into effect. No one had been hurt, or even accused. There would be time enough to test the measure when its real effect in a concrete case could be seen—after the state had had an opportunity to correct such defects as experience might disclose. The position of Justices Black and Douglas vis-à-vis that of Mr. Justice Frankfurter in the *Adler* and *Peters* cases reveals another facet of the difference between the idealistic and pragmatic approaches.

Slochower v. *Bd. of Higher Education of New York* [56] held that a state may not discharge an employee—a teacher—for asserting the privilege against self-incrimination in a congressional investigation. In the Court's view, the state had in effect converted the claim of privilege "into a conclusive presumption of guilt. Since no such inference of guilt was possible from the claim before a federal committee, the discharge falls. . . ." Justices Reed, Burton, Minton and Harlan dissented.

The problem, however, is different when a state looks into the *fitness* of a state employee for his job. Beilan, a public school teacher, refused to tell his superintendent whether he had held a position in the Communist Party and was discharged for "incompetency." Lerner, a subway conductor, was fired by New York City as a person of "doubtful trust and reliability" because of his "lack of candor" in refusing to answer questions as to membership in subversive organizations. The Court found no self-incrimination problem under the Fifth Amendment because the "federal privilege" is

[56] 350 U.S. 551 (1956).

not available in these state administrative proceedings. Both discharges were upheld as resting on reasonable findings of *unfitness*—not, as in *Slochower*, because of a Fifth Amendment plea, nor because of opinions and beliefs, nor for "security" reasons.[57] Four judges—Warren, Black, Douglas and Brennan—dissented. In Mr. Justice Black's view "We have here only a bare refusal to testify; and the Court holds that sufficient to show these employees are unfit to hold their public posts. That makes qualification for public office turn solely on a matter of belief—a notion very much at war with the Bill of Rights. . . . Our initial error in all this business (see *Dennis* v. *United States* . . .) was our disregard of the basic principle that government can concern itself only with the actions of men, not with their opinions or beliefs."

CIVIL LIBERTY—LEGISLATIVE INVESTIGATIONS

Legislatures cannot perform their functions adequately without information as to social conditions. Accordingly it is settled that the power to investigate is an inherent part of the legislative process. In modern times, however, some congressional committees appear to have abused their investigatory powers. A few years ago Mr. W. T. Gossett, Vice President and General Counsel of the Ford Motor Company, described the problem in these terms: [58]

> Congressional investigations launched for the purpose of inquiring into questions of personal conduct closely resemble the inquisitorial functions of our grand juries. As all lawyers know, in any investigation or grand jury proceeding, it is inevitable that many fruitless lines of inquiry will be undertaken. And so some false leads must be pursued. One reason for the inviolate rule of secrecy in a grand jury proceeding is the urgent necessity of protecting the good name of the many innocent persons who must be questioned and who, through no fault of their own, might be under suspicion before a determination is made as to which, if any, of those under investigation will be subjected to indictment or other action.
>
> But no such protection is accorded to those who are so unfortunate as to be required to testify before many of our congressional committees. Witnesses are questioned in public, while being denied those constitu-

[57] *Lerner* v. *Casey*, 357 U.S. 468 (1958); *Beilan* v. *Bd. of Public Education of Philadelphia*, 357 U.S. 399 (1958).

[58] *A Call to Leadership*, Ford Motor Company pamphlet.

tional safeguards which in a court proceeding are granted as a matter of right to one actually accused of a crime. The constitutional safeguards to which I refer, of course, are the rights of the accused to be informed in advance of the nature of the charges against him; his right to be confronted with the witnesses who testify against him, and to subject them to cross-examination; his right to compulsory process for obtaining witnesses in his favor; his right to be represented by counsel; and his right to testify then and there in his own defense.

A congressional investigation that delves into matters of personal conduct quickly assumes the aspect of a trial and thus abridges the rights of individuals, guaranteed by the Constitution. And there have been cases in which, as a result of the publicity of committee hearings, witnesses have been exposed to such penalties as dismissal from their jobs, loss of pension payments and lasting injury to their reputations.

Those who would defend such practices are quick to point out that a witness before a congressional committee is not in jeopardy—that is, he is not subject to a jail sentence by the committee in connection with the matter about which he is being interrogated. But the argument ignores the fact that the committee has the power, at the very least, to sully a man's reputation unmercifully, and to many men a good name is fully as important as merely being out of jail. Moreover, a committee can send a witness to jail for refusal to answer a question—even one which a court might not require him to answer.

I think it must be concluded that the current practices of investigating committees are without proper standards. Persons are now subpoenaed before such committees and afforded no right to counsel. Although they often are subjected to the most searching cross-examination themselves, they are denied the right to cross-examine those who testify against them. If they are so-called hostile witnesses, they often are not even accorded the right to make a statement—prepared or otherwise; and if the behavior of a witness is such as not to please the committee or some of its members, he can be summarily punished.

Some committee members seemingly have viewed the committee as a final court of justice sitting in judgment on the conduct of individuals appearing before the committee. Thus they usurp the judicial function. On the other hand, committee members can and do slander witnesses with impunity, secure in the knowledge that there can be no retaliation in court. . . .

In such an inquiry there is no assumption that the individual is innocent until proved guilty. There are none of the safeguards of a trial to which, by the Constitution and the law, each man is entitled. Instead, there is a type of trial by public opinion, a pillorying of individuals not accused of crimes—of individuals only suspected of being engaged in or knowing something about some improper activity. And the rules are the same whether the witness is innocent or guilty.

Though there was some initial doubt, it is now well settled that the privilege against self-incrimination applies to congressional proceedings. *Slochower's* case, moreover, demonstrates that a state may not penalize a person for asserting the privilege in a federal investigation. But society in general, one's associates, employer, and potential future employers, may see in the claim of privilege an admission of guilt. Can its true essence then be achieved by less suicidal means? Does "free speech" include the right of silence on the witness stand? If the answer must be "no" in general, perhaps it may be a qualified "yes" in conjunction with long-settled, fair-hearing principles. The rules of evidence in a judicial proceeding preclude the questioning of a witness on matters not relevant or material to an issue before the court. When relevance or materiality is doubtful, the questioner upon objection must show the propriety of his inquiry or drop it. Failure to answer appropriate questions is punishable; yet the rules of relevancy and materiality block "fishing expeditions." In this manner the public interest in obtaining evidence for law enforcement and the witness' interest in privacy are balanced in judicial hearings. A quite similar device for reconciling public and private interests in legislative investigations appears to be developing. *Watkins* v. *United States* [59] involved a witness before the House Un-American Activities Committee who did not claim the Fifth Amendment privilege, but refused to answer certain questions on the ground that they were not "pertinent to the question under inquiry." The Supreme Court reversed his contempt conviction because he "had not been adequately apprised of the subject matter of the . . . investigation or the pertinency thereto of the questions he refused to answer." [60] In short only pertinent questions must be answered. This, of course, implies that in one way or another Congress must with reasonable clarity define the scope of a committee's authority, so that witnesses and others may know what questions are pertinent and what are

[59] 354 U.S. 178 (1957).

[60] See also *Barenblatt* v. *U.S.*, 79 S. Ct. 1081 (1959); *Skull* v. *Virginia ex rel. Committee on Law Reform and Racial Activities*, 79 S. Ct. 838 (1959); *Sweezy* v. *New Hampshire*, 354 U.S. 234 (1957).

not. The future may bring further protections for the individual vis-à-vis legislative investigations, including possibly the right to counsel, confrontation, and cross-examination.

In the orthodox, long-settled view, the purpose of the privilege against self-incrimination is to block prosecution—not to prevent embarrassment. Thus, if for any reason a witness is prosecution-proof, he is not entitled to the privilege. Accordingly, a witness must testify (or suffer punishment) as to any act which, however immoral, is not illegal. The same as to any criminal act for which prosecution is barred, as for example, by a pardon or statute of limitations. On this basis Congress sometimes grants immunity from prosecution in order to get testimony otherwise not available. This device was upheld years ago, and more recently in *Ullman* v. *United States*[61] over the dissent of Justices Black and Douglas. Their view was that the "Fifth Amendment is not only a protection against conviction and prosecution but a safeguard of conscience and human dignity and freedom of expression as well." If this is to be taken literally, it means that no witness would ever have to testify on anything unless he chose to do so. This might be an excellent answer to McCarthyism, but it goes so far to the opposite extreme as seriously to impede both law-making and law-enforcement. Indeed on Mr. Justice Black's interpretation of self-incrimination the great investigations that made Senator Black famous would not have been possible.

CIVIL LIBERTY—FREEDOM OF RELIGION

The First Amendment prohibits congressional legislation "respecting an establishment of religion, or prohibiting the free exercise thereof. . . ." Both principles have been "absorbed" into the Fourteenth Amendment via the *Palko* rule. Each is plagued with difficulty. Does the restraint on establishment require a complete "separation of church and state," or does it merely outlaw preferred treatment for one, or some, religious bodies? May cities give property-tax exemption to all churches? Certainly this is impartiality, but it is not complete separation. The same may be said of most of the "released-time" systems for teaching religion in the

[61] 350 U.S. 422 (1956).

public schools. *Illinois ex rel. McCollum* v. *Bd. of Education* [62] invalidated a program which released each student from a regular class and permitted him to report either to a "study hall," or to the school room in which a church of his choosing provided denominational instruction. Later *Zorach* v. *Clauson* [63] upheld a plan essentially similar except that under it the religious instruction took place outside the schools, i.e., not in or on public property. Justices Black, Frankfurter and Jackson found the property distinction unimportant since in both situations the compulsory school attendance laws were being used, if indirectly, to add to the appeals of Sunday-School-on-a-week-day. "The greater effectiveness of this system over voluntary attendance after school," as Mr. Justice Jackson put it, "is due to the truant officer who, if the youngster fails to go to the church school, dogs him back to the public school room."

The "free exercise" problem is at least as difficult and farther reaching. "Religion" is not a term of precise content. What it entails for some is anything but religious for others. Thus the secular and the "religious" impinge upon each other endlessly. The injunction to render unto Caesar what belongs to Caesar recognizes the problem, but does not solve it. Essentially, as the Court observed in *Cantwell* v. *Connecticut*,[64] the trouble is that the First Amendment "embraces two concepts—freedom to believe and freedom to act. The first is absolute but, in the nature of things, the second cannot be." The *Flag Salute* cases [65] present the problem in perhaps its cruelest form: may a child be penalized for refusing to salute the flag as part of the public school curriculum when the salute offends his religious convictions? The Court first answered yes—and later no. Excerpts from the great opinions in these cases could not do their authors justice. Those who read them fully may want to ponder this question: did the majority (including Black) treat the second case as a problem in "free speech" because it could not effectively answer Frankfurter's dissenting view as to the meaning of "free exercise of religion"?

62 333 U.S. 203 (1948).

63 343 U.S. 306 (1952).

64 310 U.S. 296 (1940).

65 *Minersville School Dist.* v. *Gobitis,* 310 U.S. 586 (1940); *West Va. Bd. of Education* v. *Barnette,* 319 U.S. 624 (1943).

CIVIL LIBERTY—FREEDOM OF EXPRESSION

A basic weakness of dictatorship is that it relies upon the thinking power of a select few. Minds outside the inner circle are drugged into submissive stupor by all the arts that modern mass-psychology can muster—or, if need be, eliminated. Democracy's genius on the other hand is its willingness to draw upon the community's total brain power. Uncommunicated ideas serve no social and little, if any, private purpose. Without freedom of expression there is small incentive, or stimulation, for thought. The imprisoned mind decays. For these reasons the advocates of democracy stress free speech, press and assembly as the foundation of political freedom. They are the tools of society's thinking process.

Democracy then is the *unfettered exchange of ideas* with public control of *action* in accordance with those views which win acceptance, i.e., consent of the people, in the market place of reason. Long ago Judge Learned Hand pointed up the difficulty: words may be used not only as "keys of discussion," but also as "triggers" of harmful conduct. To trigger-off illegal action which the community has had no opportunity to discuss and accept or reject is the antithesis of government by consent of the governed. Falsely shouting fire in a dark and crowded theater is not calculated to start a rational discussion. Such "force words," that is, words which threaten a "clear and present danger," are not part of society's thinking process. Hence, as Holmes taught, they are not entitled to the very special protection which the First Amendment gives to "discussion words." Shouting fire in the theater is at one extreme; a graduate seminar on Beethoven is at the other. Such cases present no problems. But how shall the line be drawn in the penumbra between these two where "thought merges into action"? The difficulty is usually magnified by an irritated climate of opinion as in the Red Scare of the 1920's or the McCarthyism of the 1950's.

In *Dennis* v. *United States* [66] the accused were charged with violating the Smith Act by advocating and teaching violent overthrow of government. They defended on free-speech grounds—and lost. Mr. Justice Black dissented (as did Mr. Justice Douglas):

[66] 341 U.S. 494 (1951).

> I have always believed that the First Amendment is the keystone of our government, that the freedoms it guarantees provide the best insurance against destruction of all freedom. At least as to speech in the realm of public matters, I believe that the "clear and present danger" test does not "mark the furthermost boundaries of protected expression" but does "no more than recognize a minimum compulsion of the Bill of Rights."

Obviously the Justice goes beyond Holmes' danger test. In the area of public matters at least he seems to approach the principle of absolute free speech. It is noteworthy that those judges who *upheld* the *Dennis* conviction recognized that the conduct in question had posed no immediate danger.

Mr. Justice Frankfurter concurred with the majority. He could not treat discourse as a monolithic thing of fungible nature. The Holmes-Hand distinction between "discussion words" and "force words" is not the only relevant distinction. "Not every type of speech occupies the same position on the scale of values. There is no substantial public interest in permitting . . . 'the lewd and obscene, the profane, the libelous, and the insulting or 'fighting' words—those by their very utterance inflict injury or tend to incite an immediate breach of the peace'. . . . We have frequently indicated that the interest in protecting speech depends on the circumstances of the occasion. It is pertinent to the decision before us to consider where on the scale of values we have in the past placed the type of speech now claiming constitutional immunity." Then, finding that conspiratorial teaching and advocacy of violent overthrow of government "ranks low" "[o]n any scale of values which we have hitherto recognized," the Justice considered the interests which Congress had found at stake on the other side of the scale—national self-preservation, vis-à-vis the communist menace. On balance he could not say that Congress in the Smith Act had gone beyond the real of reason. To inquire further as to the wisdom of what the legislative body had done seemed an intrusion into the legislative domain.

This again is the so-called reasonable-man test. It means in essence that when constitutional issues are not free from doubt—when the problem is one on which reasonable men may disagree—the view taken by the elected branches of government must be upheld. In short, doubt is to be resolved in favor of democratic self-government. Mr. Justice Frankfurter seems to believe that democracy cannot thrive, cannot develop respect and self-confidence, if it is not free to work out its own problems, *at least* in the area where solutions are not so clear as to be beyond debate by reasonable men. Mr. Justice Black's view, on the other hand, seems to assume that democracy cannot thrive unless it has *special* court protection.

Difficulty increases when contending claims are more evenly matched than were those in the *Dennis* case. Freedom of the press is a crucial constitutional right and so is a fair trial. What is the Court to do when such basic interests collide, as when newspaper editorials put pressure upon a trial judge or jury in pending litigation? Powerful arguments may be made on both sides, but surely the Constitution does not spell out an answer. If general propositions are to be decisive, which one shall it be—FREE SPEECH, or FAIR TRIAL? Is the intensity of a judge's regard for one or the other to determine the result? Such were the difficulties presented in *Times-Mirror* v. *Superior Court of California.*[67] Mr. Justice Black, speaking for the Court, did not openly assert that freedom of the press is more important than a fair trial. Yet unavowedly he made that appraisal by resorting to the clear and present danger test, whose avowed purpose is to give utterance a preferred status. Having chosen his legal ground, he then *reappraised* the facts of the case and found no imminent danger.

Mr. Justice Frankfurter dissented. Finding no plain answer in the Constitution, he could not pretend, explicitly or otherwise, that one was there. The power of courts to safeguard the administration of justice from outside pressures is an ancient tradition. Even First Amendment freedoms depend to some extent upon protection by fair trials. And so, finding no special circumstances to remove all doubt, the Justice would not intrude upon a state's decision to give priority to the trial—or, presumably, to the press. In this view, different jurisdictions would be free to try different solutions for the vexing problem of "trial by newspaper." Experience so gained would nourish both the judicial and the legislative processes. Such is the implication of Holmes' pragmatic teaching that the life of the law is not logic, but experience.

Are there cases in which Mr. Justice Frankfurter is prepared to override a legislative choice of values? In *Sweezy* v. *New Hamp-*

[67] 314 U.S. 252 (1941).

shire [68] a state un-American activities "committee" had questioned a citizen about the origins and supporters of the Progressive Party. He responded that he knew of no communist connection therewith. Then he refused to answer further on the ground that the questions "infringed upon the inviolability of the right to privacy in his political thoughts, actions and associations." In a concurring opinion Mr. Justice Frankfurter found merit in these claims:

For a citizen to be made to forego even a part of so basic a liberty as his political autonomy, the subordinating interest of the State must be compelling. . . . [The] inviolability of privacy belonging to a citizen's political loyalties has so overwhelming an importance to the well-being of our kind of society that it cannot be constitutionally encroached upon on the basis of so meagre a countervailing interest of the State as may be argumentatively found in the remote, shadowy threat to the security of New Hampshire allegedly presented in the origins and contributing elements of the Progressive Party and in petitioner's relations to these. . . . Whatever, on the basis of massive proof and in the light of history, of which this Court may well take judicial notice, be the justification for not regarding the Communist Party as a conventional political party, no such justification has been afforded in regard to the Progressive Party. A foundation in fact and reason would have to be established far weightier than the intimations that appear in the record to warrant such a view of the Progressive Party. . . .

To be sure, this is a conclusion based on a judicial judgment in balancing two contending principles—the right of a citizen to political privacy, as protected by the Fourteenth Amendment, and the right of the State to self-protection. And striking the balance implies the exercise of judgment. This is the inescapable judicial task in giving substantive content, legally enforced, to the Due Process Clause, and it is a task ultimately committed to this Court. It must not be an exercise of whim or will. It must be an overriding judgment founded on something much deeper and more justifiable than personal preference. As far as it lies within human limitations, it must be an impersonal judgment. It must rest on fundamental presuppositions rooted in history to which widespread acceptance may fairly be attributed. Such a judgment must be arrived at in a spirit of humility when it counters the judgment of the State's highest court. But, in the end, judgment cannot be escaped—the judgment of this Court.

[68] 354 U.S. 234 (1957).

It will be noted that the Justice did not pretend his conclusion is literally prescribed in the Constitution. He rests rather on "fundamental presuppositions rooted in history to which widespread acceptance may fairly be attributed." These for him illuminate the written words. Or, as he put it in *Sweezy's* case, "While the language of the Constitution does not change, the changing circumstances of a progressive society for which it was designed yield new and fuller import to its meaning." Perhaps this would have pleased Thomas Reed Powell, who in his final summation observed that what he "most objected to in many judges is something that springs from a feeling of judicial duty to try to make out that their conclusions come from the Constitution."

The *Dennis* case, perhaps, may be classified as one in which a relatively weak private interest collided with a major public interest. Such at least was the legislative appraisal, and Mr. Justice Frankfurter could not find it so unreasonable as to warrant judicial intervention. In *Sweezy* at the other extreme, the Justice found a formidable private, vis-à-vis an amorphous public, interest. The discrepancy seemed so great that he could not find a contrary legislative appraisal within the bounds of reason. And so with obvious misgiving he voted, as he rarely does in such cases, against the state's position. The *Times-Mirror* case perhaps falls somewhere between these two extremes. There the Justice found the contending claims—fair trial versus free press—so evenly balanced as to preclude judicial intrusion upon what the state had done.

No doubt this judicial balancing of interests—more accurately, this sitting in judgment upon balances struck by others—is dangerous business, not designed for small men. Yet it is inevitable on Mr. Justice Frankfurter's premise that judicial review is a historic duty, even though the old eighteenth century Constitution speaks with less than crystal clarity on some twentieth century problems. Mr. Justice Black cannot accept the second part of his colleague's premise. For him the Constitution is perfectly clear at least as to utterance on public matters. The First Amendment forbids laws "abridging the freedom of speech, or of the press. . . ." There are no explicit qualifications. Nor is this a matter of casual or passing significance. The verbal clarity of the Constitution and the importance of the interests involved are Mr. Justice Black's shield against critics who charge him with ignoring the special facts of each particular case. Those to whom the ancient document speaks less plainly cannot otherwise explain how he always reaches the same result regardless of the facts involved. As Mr. Justice Jackson expressed it in *Terminiello's* case: the libertarians reverse "this conviction by reiterating generalized approbations of freedom of speech with which, in the abstract, no one will disagree. Doubts as to their applicability are lulled by avoidance of more than passing reference to the circumstance of Terminiello's speech and judging it as if he had spoken . . . to empty benches. . . ."[69] The background of this case is worth noting. Terminiello, a suspended priest, was introduced by the notorious Gerald L. K. Smith and spoke in a Chicago auditorium to about 800 persons gathered under the auspices of the Christian Veterans of America. His speech, according to Mr. Justice Jackson—just back from the Nuremberg trials—"followed, with fidelity that is more than coincidental, the pattern of European fascist leaders." Linking Democrats, Jews and Communists in a common conspiracy, it reeked with racial hatred. Outside a protesting crowd of some 1000 persons—Communist led, according to Terminiello—milled about in unconcealed hostility. Police were unable to prevent several outbursts of violence including the smashing of doors and windows. Mr. Justice Jackson saw in this episode a struggle between "totalitarian groups" for what the Nazis called "the conquest of the streets" as the "key to power." Like Mr. Justice Frankfurter, he could not believe that this was the free discussion, the tool of democracy, which the First Amendment's unqualified language was meant to safeguard.

It is not quite accurate to suggest that Mr. Justice Black always discounts every consideration which might limit discourse. He spoke for the Court in *Gibbony* v. *Empire Storage & Ice Co.*[70] This involved an injunction against picketing calculated to force the company to violate a state anti-trust law. The Justice upheld the injunction, though he insists that picketing is a modern form of free speech:

> The policy against restraints of trade is of long standing. . . . It is clearly drawn in an attempt to afford all persons an equal opportunity to buy goods. There was clear danger, imminent and immediate, that

[69] *Terminiello* v. *Chicago,* 337 U.S. 1, 13 (1949).
[70] 336 U.S. 490 (1949).

unless restrained, [the picketers] would succeed in making that policy a dead letter. . . . [Their] power along with that of their allies was irresistible. And it is clear that [they] were doing more than exercising a right of free speech or press.

Here was a clash between utterance and a more mundane interest in which Mr. Justice Black for once held in favor of the mundane. The decisive element of course was his finding that the picketers had engaged in "more" than mere discourse. No doubt, but was nothing more than discourse involved in the *Dennis, Times-Mirror* and *Terminiello* cases? More, that is, which democratic government may fairly take into account? In *Dennis* Mr. Justice Black insisted quite accurately that the conspiracy there charged was conspiracy to "advocate and teach" communist ideals, not to incite overthrow of government. Mr. Justice Frankfurter agreed, but thought that "it would be equally wrong to treat [the conduct in question] as a seminar in political theory." Where nothing but discussion is involved there is no difficulty. For most judges the constant quandary in these cases is that they involve something more. In this view the problem is to find the point at which words become merely a mask for fraud or force.

CIVIL LIBERTY—RACIAL DISCRIMINATION

If the Great Depression left its mark upon constitutional law, so doubtless did the Nazis. Hitler's Storm Troops demonstrated the implications of racial discrimination in terms that no one could ignore. Just as the new Court discarded the old Substantive Due Process and Dual Federalism in favor of first principles, so it rejected separate-but-equal of the same vintage and returned to the spirit of *Strauder* and *Ex parte Virginia*.[71] The "corrupt bargain" of *Reunion and Reaction* had outlived its day. Having mastered mass production, America turned from the special interests of businessmen to the general interests which all men have in common: a more bountiful enjoyment of civil liberty and the fruits of industrial know-how.

Perhaps because crisis was not so immediate in the racial realm, the Court moved more gradually there than in the area of economics. At first it simply insisted upon real, as distinct from the

[71] These cases are discussed in Chap. IV, above.

traditional mock equality of separate-but-equal.[72] For the first time in history the second half of the *Plessy* formula was vigorously enforced. Then, having laid this ground-work, the Court responded *unanimously* to the conscience of America. The Jeffersonian dream of human freedom and equality again prevailed. In the context of our times racial segregation and equality were found incompatible in public schols,[73] public beaches and bathhouses,[74] municipal golf courses,[75] parks [76] and buses.[77] Obviously little or none of *Plessy* v. *Ferguson* remains.

Many who resist "integration" resent the persistent efforts of the National Association for the Advancement of Colored People (NAACP) to secure enforcement of the Fourteenth and Fifteenth Amendments. This resistance has found expression in state efforts to destroy that organization by requiring it to disclose the names of its members—obviously for the purpose of exposing them to harassment. The validity of one such effort came before the Court in *NAACP* v. *Alabama*.[78] The state argued on the authority of *Bryant* v. *Zimmerman* [79] which had sustained a New York law requiring the Ku Klux Klan to disclose its members' names. The Court found a difference in the two situations based on the Klan's well known activities "involving acts of unlawful intimidation and violence." It was also pointed out that the NAACP had "made an uncontroverted showing that on past occasions revelation of the identity of its rank-and-file members has exposed these members to economic reprisal, loss of employment, threat of physical coercion, and other manifestations of public hostility." Under these conditions the Court held unanimously that the Alabama measure was an invasion of freedom of association, in violation of the Fourteenth Amendment.

[72] See, for example, *Missouri ex rel. Gaines* v. *Canada*, 305 U.S. 337 (1938); *Sweatt* v. *Painter*, 339 U.S. 629 (1950).

[73] *Brown* v. *Topeka*, 347 U.S. 483 (1954).

[74] *Dawson* v. *Mayor of Baltimore*, 220 F. 2d 386 (1955), affirmed 350 U.S. 877 (1955).

[75] *Holmes* v. *Atlanta*, 223 F. 2d. 93 (1955), reversed 350 U.S. 879 (1955).

[76] *New Orleans City Parks* v. *Detiege*, 252 F. 2d. 122 (1958), affirmed 358 U.S. 54 (1958).

[77] *Browder* v. *Gayle*, 142 F. Supp. 707 (1956), affirmed 352 U.S. 903 (1956).

[78] 357 U.S. 449 (1958).

[79] 278 U.S. 63 (1928).

Another common anti-NAACP device is one prohibiting organized support of litigation as "barratry." The purpose obviously is to prevent the NAACP from assisting victims of discrimination in law suits which they could not individually afford. The counterpart of this approach was the largely successful resistance to the Civil Rights Bill of 1957. That measure would have authorized the federal Department of Justice to litigate for protection of a wide range of civil rights. If the poor cannot organize to protect themselves by litigation, and if government may not litigate to protect them, of what value are their constitutional rights? Or as the ancient common law dictum has it: without a remedy there is no right.

VII

EPILOGUE

The American way of life is not a simple concept, resting as it does upon Hamiltonian materialism and the spiritual grandeur of the Jeffersonian tradition. No wonder outsiders, and sometimes we ourselves, are confused:

> The animating principle of [Jeffersonianism] has been the belief that the average man can be trusted with freedom and responsibility, that he does not require the guidance of an authoritarian church or of a privileged aristocracy or bureaucracy, and that whenever he finds adequate opportunity for exercising initiative, hidden talents and energies will be released for constructive purposes. . . .
>
> Yet although this faith has been the distinguishing feature of American civilization, and although it has been affirmed by all those statesmen and intellectuals who have been most characteristically American, it has never been accepted by all Americans, nor has it [fully] permeated the American mind or found [unrivaled] expression in American systems of thought. Much of American history has been a conflict between the American ideal of democracy and the European attitudes of class privilege and government by an elite [especially in the economic area]. And when America has failed, it has usually been because it has not been true to its own genius but has been too much influenced by doctrines and precedents derived from Europe. The most notable example of this tendency was the Federalist and Hamiltonian politico-economic system, which was deliberately copied from European models and . . . based on a European belief in a ruling class and distrust of democracy.[1]

[1] Henry B. Parkes, *The American Experience* (New York, Knopf, 1955), pp. 337–338.

While we had the Great Frontier, it was not too difficult to cherish freedom and opportunity for all men and at the same time to exalt private wealth and power. But the free lands of the West are no longer there to cushion the abuses of Hamiltonianism. America has moved from the frontier to the city, from farm to factory. We have sacrificed individual or family independence to a vast, impersonal industrial order. Minute specialization and division of labor bind us to one another in an endless web of mutual interdependence. Who among us does not rely upon unknown mercenaries for the production of his food, clothing and medicine —to say nothing of the luxuries of life? We depend upon services that spring not from love, friendship or sympathy, but from the most brittle, the most readily corruptible of human motives: the hope of pecuniary gain. Society, once incoherent yet homogenous, is now a "coherent heterogeneity." Our world is a world of organized capital, organized labor and organized everything else; of corporations, trade associations, partnerships, unions, pressure groups, societies, parties, factions, clubs, committees and all the rest. We are a nation of joiners—of organizational men—because in our complex industrial system the individual cannot otherwise survive. The impersonal forces of mass production are too great, too remote and too complex to be controlled by disunited individualism. We live in a Hamiltonian world and dream Jeffersonian dreams.

But dreams may be the most potent forces in life. We have turned to government and what Walter Rauschenbush called its "superior Christian ethics" to save us from unmitigated Hamiltonianism. The service, or welfare state, now implements the Jeffersonian ideal: the integrity and well-being of Everyman vis-à-vis material forces beyond the power of individual control. The means have changed, but not the end.

The world is now divided between Soviet materialism and the spiritual aspirations of the Greco-Hebraic tradition with its oriental counterparts. Those who are not already committed to the Soviet—and doubtless some who are—are troubled by the apparent dichotomy of our position. The spread of neutralism among those who still have a choice reflects at least in part their estimate of the relative importance of Hamiltonianism and Jeffersonianism in American culture.

In this context the Supreme Court plays its role. Without purse or sword, its only power is the power to persuade—which is to say it can succeed only to the extent that it confirms what for the time is deepest in our hearts and minds. If it has shifted from age to age, it has done so in response to our changing ideal and material commitments. From Marshall to Taney and Waite, then back to Field, and thence to Holmes and the "new" Court, is a swing in the pendulum of history back and forth between Hamiltonianism and Jeffersonianism. We may hope it is not smugness which sees in this the nourishing heart-beat of the American way of life. Some deem it the indecisive vacillation of a people that cannot make up its mind—a people whose ideals serve merely to assuage the conscience, while conduct takes more earthy forms.

Moved, no doubt, by the suicide of the pre-depression economic order and the Age of Dictators, the Supreme Court is now thoroughly Jeffersonian in its values. In crisis after crisis, we return to the abiding values of the spirit. But the Justices are divided on method: how far shall the Court go in wet-nursing democracy (as the old Court wet-nursed Hamiltonianism); to what extent shall it hold back and permit the American Dream to develop its own *democratic* devices of responsibility and self-confidence? Never before on the bench has the problem of the judicial role in our federated democracy been canvassed with such articulate, intellectual vigor. There, one ventures, posterity may find unique greatness in the "new" Supreme Court.

TABLE OF CASES

INDEX